Igniting School Performance

Also by Vincent F. Cotter
Performance Is Key: Connecting the Links to Leadership and Excellence

Igniting School Performance

A Pathway from Academic Paralysis to Excellence

Dr. Vincent F. Cotter

ROWMAN & LITTLEFIELD
Lanham • Boulder • New York • London

Published by Rowman & Littlefield
An imprint of The Rowman & Littlefield Publishing Group, Inc.
4501 Forbes Boulevard, Suite 200, Lanham, Maryland 20706
www.rowman.com

6 Tinworth Street, London SE11 5AL, United Kingdom

Copyright © 2019 by Vincent F. Cotter

All rights reserved. No part of this book may be reproduced in any form or by any electronic or mechanical means, including information storage and retrieval systems, without written permission from the publisher, except by a reviewer who may quote passages in a review.

British Library Cataloguing in Publication Information Available

Library of Congress Control Number: 2019949839

ISBN 978-1-4758-5213-4 (cloth)
ISBN 978-1-4758-5214-1 (paper)
ISBN 978-1-4758-5215-8 (electronic)

Contents

Foreword — vii
Dr. Robert D. Hassler

Preface — ix

Introduction — xiii

PART I: BUILDING THE FIRE — 1

1. The Commitment to Performance — 3
2. Performance-Focused Leadership — 13
3. Principles of Performance — 17

PART II: IGNITING THE FIRE — 27

4. Building Performance Chemistry — 29
5. The Transition to Higher Performance — 39
6. Guiding the Process — 49

PART III: FANNING THE FLAMES — 61

7. Implementation Strategies for Success — 63
8. Sustaining Performance — 71
9. Case Studies — 81

   Conclusion — 97

PART IV: APPENDICES **101**

Appendix A: Performance Instruments and Tools 103

Appendix B: Leadership Development Exercises 123

Notes 133

Bibliography 137

About the Author 141

Foreword

Few educators have actually improved student achievement scores by double digits over a five-year period and sustained that growth until all schools reached or exceeded the 85th percentile in proficiency. There are also even fewer leaders that have designed a plan for improving performance which remains in effect some twenty years later. While these accomplishments are certainly significant, author Vincent F. Cotter claims that these results are possible for every school, district, and student. Clearly a bold statement but let me explain why I believe that he is "dead-on."

From the outset, Dr. Cotter recognizes the importance of engaging all stakeholders in the process. Second, there is recognition of a leader's role in producing such results and possessing the skills to do so. Third, there is an understanding of the commitment, the passion, and the courage that is necessary to pursue an agenda which focuses on higher performance.

By unleashing the power of stakeholders to engage in the process of improvement, the journey can easily become a risky endeavor for one's leadership and is not for the "faint of heart." Having the ability to understand the dynamics of an organization, identify its disconnections, and develop a plan based on proven principles can alleviate the risk, minimize turmoil, and lower the frustration level of such a venture. Understanding how to develop an authentic and sustainable improvement process without internal disruption is the key to this approach.

Having walked through the "mine fields" of change and reform, Dr. Cotter provides a straightforward approach to the improvement equation by providing principles and strategies, which harness the imagination of all stakeholders to one of higher performance for all students. His plan for improvement is compelling, realistic, and attainable.

Building on his first book, *Performance Is Key*, the practitioner or aspiring leader learns how to skillfully create support for higher performing schools by empowering stakeholders and having all participants engage in achieving the desired outcomes and sharing in the responsibility for their execution. What makes Dr. Cotter's design even more unique is his ability to link basic theory to practice through personal vignettes and experiences which connect all stakeholders to the important contributions that they are capable of providing.

Dr. Cotter's plea to eliminate underperforming schools is inspirational. Many educators have the academic background and knowledge, but few also have the practical experience of knowing what works along with a proven track record of improving learning for *ALL* students. This publication will not only complement any school or district's reform efforts but also propel them to a higher level of performance.

I agree, "Just OK" schools are no longer "good enough" and to reach higher performance levels educational leaders must have the skill to facilitate a process of high expectations. For those seeking those skills, *Igniting School Performance* will guide you to excellence and higher performance outcomes.

Dr. Robert D. Hassler
Retired Superintendent of Schools
Exemplary Schools Organization, Co-founder
Consultant
Author

Preface

IS STUDENT ACHIEVEMENT STILL IMPORTANT?

Sounds like a crazy question? Not really when one considers the lack of outrage over the recently released 2018 NAEP scores which indicated that overall student achievement scores were "flat." Over a number of years, NAEP, considered the nation's barometer of student achievement, has reported miniscule gains particularly in the area of Reading and Mathematics.[1]

To be accurate, there were some areas of the test which suggested some promise but from this perspective, the growth was not "Good Enough" and frankly, we cannot settle for "Good Enough" when it comes to educating *ALL children* in this country.

Interestingly, while researchers such as Eric A. Hanushek "have linked the quality of student performance to the economic growth in the country,"[2] it appears that leaders fail to recognize the seriousness of the issue. Based on PISA results, many countries with fewer resources have "leap frogged" U.S. performance.[3] Additionally, with the global implementation of technology and the integration of those technologies into worldwide educational systems, the knowledge curve was "flattened" which accelerated educational growth for those countries with the vision to invest in education and for those that made achievement a priority. Simply put, we are losing our economic and intellectual advantage in the world, making us less competitive.

Compounding the issue of stagnant student performance is the fact that it comes at a time when the projected impact of Artificial Intelligence requires a highly educated and trained populace with critical thinking, problem-solving, and technical skills necessitating adaptation and innovation. Further illustrating the skill gap is a recent report that mathematics scores have dropped to a twenty-year low on the American College Test (ACT).[4]

On the surface, all educational leaders state that of course student achievement is the priority of the school or school district but privately many leaders indicate that they are overwhelmed with mandates, minutiae, and a myriad of operational issues which take priority over focusing on student achievement. Others indicate that in fulfilling state mandates associated with teacher performance, the student achievement issue will resolve itself. Obviously, in reviewing student performance results by state, it is clear that the implementation of any one program to solve a problem as complex as underachievement is not the answer. Conversely, layering programs on top of each other or a combining of unconnected programs is also not the answer.

Without question there are many interrelated layers to the achievement challenge which require an in-depth examination. To peel back the layers of the "achievement onion," take a moment to examine the organization's alignment to its goals, outcomes, and resource allocation. Ask yourself if a culture of continuous improvement has been nurtured? Is there an internal attitude that is committed to overcoming obstacles? Is your staff willing to persevere until it meets the organization's achievement goals or does it seek excuses for its poor performance?

Additionally, accountability systems must reflect the values of the organization. Remember, what gets measured gets done! Finally, as a leader, do you have the "will" and the courage to facilitate the change necessary to meet the achievement challenge?

All schools have the internal capacity to reach higher performance levels. One need not look further than one's own staff and leadership team to identify the talent to get the job done. Having observed low-income schools with few resources reach amazingly high levels of student performance demonstrates that it is not all about funding and certainly not about gimmicks. We also know that excuses will not deliver better outcomes. It is really all about instructional focus and finding the gaps in the interrelated elements of alignment, attitude, accountability, and leadership.

Igniting School Performance *is about understanding the importance of creating synergy between all stakeholders and committing each group to excellence. It is about you as a leader understanding the fundamentals to higher performance and flawlessly executing them. It is about the process and possessing the skills to make a difference in the performance of each child entrusted to you.*

Igniting School Performance *will provide each leader with a proven framework, guidelines and principles to transform each school or district into one capable of producing graduates that have the skills to compete on a national or international level. Strategic and synergistic strategies will release the untapped internal organizational energy to disrupt the status quo and break through the paralysis of underperformance.*

Now is the time to cast aside maintaining the status quo, to stop playing it safe, and to begin a journey toward higher performance in each and every school.

Igniting School Performance *will assist ALL stakeholders to accept the challenge of higher performance and to "step outside" one's comfort zone to improve achievement.*

Now is the time to combine leadership skill and execution with a synergistic strategy to attain sustainable improvement and higher performance.

Many leaders can move an organization forward but real leaders keep moving the organization toward an "ever changing" horizon. Imagine what is possible. Develop a plan to reach it but never become complacent when you have arrived at the destination. Stimulating imagination, synergizing stakeholders, building trust in the process, and executing a plan do not happen in isolation, but they will happen with strong synergistic and "synergetic" leadership.

Remember, as a leader, that it is insight, acquired knowledge, technical skills, and strategic facilitation that *"Ignites School Performance!"*

Igniting School Performance will provide you with the essentials to not only spark performance but nourish it until that spark becomes a blaze illuminating a pathway that will take *ALL* stakeholders on a journey to prepare *ALL* children for a future that yet remains undefined but clearly one that requires *ALL* students to be highly prepared to meet it.

Introduction

"Try Not. DO or Do Not. There is no try!"
—*Yoda*, Star Wars: The Empire Strikes Back

Igniting School Performance begins with a simple question. What kind of school do you want for the children in your neighborhood, town, city, or county? While the question is a good starting point, other questions such as: Are you willing to make a commitment so that all schools are high performing? How do you define high performing? and How might that goal be accomplished? are equally important.

From the outset of this text, there is a focus on involving all stakeholders in the process of improving student achievement and providing an inclusive leadership approach that breaks the internal paralysis or ineptness which contributes to the ongoing status quo of underachievement in far too many schools.

Stakeholders such as board members might declare that they are interested in schools that serve their community. Superintendents might focus on schools that create individuals with the desire to be life-long learners. Teachers might indicate that schools are a place where children learn. Parents may simply express that they want the schools to be good. Further qualifying each of these responses may also yield descriptions of schools that are very different from those previously described.

If you were to press each stakeholder to further expound on the criteria of a school in which they were willing to have children attend, responses might also include statements about discipline, respect, good teaching, tolerance, acceptance, involvement, and learning. Parents also want staff and faculty to recognize the positive characteristics of each child. Each of these descriptions is a "given" if a school or district is considered good.

We have many good schools in the United States. Students learn, participate in activities, and are generally happy. Parents generally appear satisfied. A bigger question for these schools is, What exactly are students learning? Are they prepared to succeed at the postsecondary level or in the global market place? Are they being challenged each and every day in school or are they simply marking time until they graduate? A more probing question might be: How does our school compare to others on a national level? or What would make our school exemplary?

We also have many failing schools in the United States, schools in which a large percentage of the student body functions below proficiency levels on reading, writing, math, and science. Unfortunately, each year thousands of students graduate without the prerequisite skills to succeed. The impact of this poorly educated population on the nation and the country's global competitiveness is staggering.[1]

We also have some of the best and brightest students in the world. These students can compete with any group of students from anywhere. For the moment they will keep the United States from falling into an economic abyss by creating and innovating, but they alone cannot keep us globally competitive or economically viable. We are stronger when all members of our society are learners and contributors.

For long-term prosperity we need ALL children to achieve at a higher level. Equity cannot be equated with mediocrity but rather equity must be synonymous with excellence and high standards. Equity is not leveling expectations to the middle but lifting everyone above the norm. Real equity involves a focus on what is being taught, how it is taught, and assessing defined skills and outcomes necessary for success in a global economy.

Students in the middle have long been overlooked and underserved. Many schools and school districts located in economically challenged areas have few Honors and Advanced Placement/International Baccalaureate courses and if they do, the enrollment numbers are low. Too many students just "go through the motions" each day and graduate with rudimentary skills. Supporting and maintaining this type of performance is tantamount to professional fraud.

Igniting School Performance *is a departure from the "Good Enough" paradigm by setting the bar high for performance standards and results. It further defines what an exemplary school looks like and provides an instrument to informally assess a school or district's instructional status. It further encourages stakeholders to create schools that exhibit the following criteria:*

- *curriculum content is highly challenging and is infused with the concepts of abstraction, problem solving.*
- *subject content requires technological competence and linguistic capability at all levels.*

- *students write in every class, every day.*
- *research is a regular activity in every class.*
- *assignments are challenging and require inferential thinking skills.*
- *learning options are flexible so as to enhance enrichment opportunities.*
- *individualization and differentiation are the norm.*
- *support programs such as tutoring and assistance abound.*
- *"state of the art" methodology and student engagement are pervasive.*
- *interdisciplinary instruction, departmental and grade level collaboration are perceived as normal outgrowths of good planning, teaching, and learning.*
- *faculty members are empowered.*
- *creativity and experimentation are encouraged.*
- *results and outcomes are expectations but responsibility for growth and progress is shared.*
- *vocational/technical education is linked to higher level academics and course work.*
- *students routinely demonstrate learning via projects, presentations, discussions, and written forms of expression.*

When such performance criteria are embedded into the teaching and learning process the instructional culture is driven to succeed. Results such as the student body scoring above 85% percentile in mathematics, reading, writing, and science tests becomes the norm. Being competitive on national and even international standardized testing (i.e., NAEP, SAT, ACT, PISA, etc.) becomes an expectation.

Moving an organization to embrace such skill sets and high standards for ALL students is the underlying challenge of *Igniting School Performance*. Clearly, it is a daunting task as evidenced by the myriad of underperforming schools that each year are classified as failing by state assessment results, but it begs the question as to why these schools cannot make progress. *Igniting School Performance* goes beyond the obvious and examines the systemic systems that influence performance.

In tackling the challenge of elevating student achievement, Igniting School Performance *is cognizant of the difficulty of breaking through the self-perpetuating dynamics of the organization with its tendency to resist change and maintain the "status quo." Therefore, much of its content is devoted to developing a process that cultivates trust and collaboration among its stakeholders.*

Igniting School Performance recognizes that persuading stakeholders to commit to high levels of performance is not easy but it is essential. Taking a stand and shifting the mindset of the organization requires courage. Only when the organization's leadership and its stakeholders fully commit to a mantra of equity and excellence for ALL students will real substantive change become transformational.

Through concrete, proven strategies, Igniting School Performance *takes the leader on a journey from acquiring stakeholder commitment for higher performance to a process which transforms the focus of an organization by embedding principles and structures into its very fabric with real sustainability.*

In this text, the challenges associated with improving performance are validated through illustrated experiential situations. Each situation correlates to proven leadership theory and is linked to a practical recommendation. While change can be a high-risk venture for a leader, strategies are provided to minimize it.

Finally, Igniting School Performance *provides Cases Studies for an educational leader to emulate and activities on which to build internal capacity and further stakeholder commitment.*

Higher student achievement is not a dream but rather a reality that we must all embrace. Better outcomes will not occur overnight but with a performance plan that values improved performance, the growth will be steady and strong.

In football it is important to, "that it was important to go long but plan to get there one yard at a time." Begin your planning today, utilize the enclosed activities and ensure your children's future tomorrow! Let's not just try, let's make it happen!

Part I

BUILDING THE FIRE

"*Schools are full of good players. Collegiality is about getting them to play together.*"
—Roland Barth

Much like the world, the fabric of any organization is continually in flux. The social, economic, and demographic influences on a school or district rarely remain the same and the impact of those changes requires a more flexible, inclusive, and proactive leadership style which builds trust in its strategic response to those changes. While strong leadership will always remain a constant, it is not only how a leader exerts his/her influence on the organization and those executing its direction but also how the leader facilitates the desired outcome without losing control of the objective.

    The chapters in Part I highlight an overall approach that will not only transform the culture of the organization to one that is focused on performance but will create a dynamic environment capable of sustaining high performance outcomes. With an adherence to the principles highlighted in this section, the school or district will demonstrate proven practices that will encourage the staff to maximize their own individual potential and to collaborate as members of a team to maximize the learning potential of ALL children.

Chapter 1

The Commitment to Performance

STAKEHOLDERS PARALYSIS

Much like building a fire, igniting performance requires climatic conditions that are conducive to change. Mobilizing all of the organizational components in a manner that supports higher performance and develops stakeholder consensus moves the organization toward higher performance. It sounds simple in theory but given the state of student achievement and the large percentage of failing schools in the nation, the challenge is formidable. In reality, a major obstacle is often the established "mind set" within each organization that is reinforced and perpetuated by those leading it.

From a cross-section of thousands of professionals at several professional conferences over a two-year period, the challenge of committing to higher performance outcomes is highlighted below.

School Board of Directors

At a National School Boards Association Conference in San Antonio, Texas, an overwhelming concern expressed to us by school board members was the question of how to address stagnant or poor student achievement in a school or a school district. Some board members were even concerned that any internal dialogue about student achievement to other board members or the superintendent might actually upset the "apple cart" of existing relationships and plunge the school or district into conflict and dysfunction.

While certainly the importance of having a functional board that has a positive relationship with the superintendent is highly desirable, it is also a widely held belief that having a dialogue about achievement and maintaining a positive relationship are not mutually exclusive of each other. It's a conversation that should not be avoided but rather embraced because each student's future depends on it. In low to middle income families, public education is often the only option for developing real tangible skills to access post-secondary programs or to obtain job training. In many cases it is really the great equalizer in the "American Dream."

To reach higher performance levels all stakeholders must discuss it with integrity and mutual respect. At the same time, it should be recognized that discussing student achievement among board members and the superintendent is really one of charting the future. The discussion must be transparent and collaborative which can create a degree of defensiveness and discomfort. It is not about micromanaging a district or political posturing but rather it is one of developing a constructive direction for improvement and aligning the resources to do it.

Planning for higher performance is a focused investment in the human potential of a district without the disruption or the turmoil of meaningless change. Some might say, Why? I'd rather choose to say, Why Not! I'd prefer to say that it is not about Excuses but rather Solutions! It is about working together in a strategic and synergistic manner.

School board members are encouraged to enjoin all stakeholders on the journey toward higher performance. It is not about blame or the past but rather collaborative problem solving. It is the essence of a team working toward the expected and entrusted goal of higher performance. The community should expect the board to partner in supporting a design and a plan that will produce improved performance.

Performance and results are part of the board's responsibility to monitor outcomes. How a school board addresses its responsibility to partner with stakeholders and monitor outcomes will determine its legacy and those that it serves. How a board views its role regarding achievement will define the district and those that it serves for years to come.

School Administrators

In Houston, Texas, at the American Association of School Administrators National Conference, when superintendents were asked if they were leading a major district wide student achievement initiative, they resoundingly indicated that it wasn't their priority. Major issues with funding or managing the school board consumed their day. They explained that they were accountable to the school board and that from their perspective the board was more interested in issues that had a more immediate impact on the district. The board simply did not promote an agenda related to achievement.

Several superintendents also indicated that they had purchased programs to remedy student achievement efforts, but rarely did they take the lead in coordinating a comprehensive effort. Other superintendents believed that they were improving, but it was clear that those efforts were "window dressing."

Unfortunately, the aforementioned superintendent's role only reinforces the status quo and is not one of growth toward higher performance. Frankly, it was unclear whether they feared the accountability associated with results or if the district ever expected better results. Tragically, this operational "mind set" contributes to the "national stagnation of achievement that is represented in the 2018 NAEP scores."[1] It is "mind set" that represents a lack of leadership and an abdication of moral responsibility.

Sidestepping one's primary responsibility to improve student performance will not generate better results. Redirecting this type of leadership requires pressure exerted from other stakeholders on the organization. Such pressure demands improvement from its leadership and forces them to develop a real plan that generates higher performance.

In taking the instructional point position in the improvement process, superintendents have a tremendous opportunity to motivate, inspire, and model transformational strategies. To convince all stakeholders that the journey to higher performance is a venture which will involve organizational shifts, the superintendent must be a strategic and synergistic leader.

Teachers

Title I, Part A of the Elementary and Secondary Education Act, as amended (ESEA) provides "financial assistance to local educational agencies (LEA's) with high numbers or percentages from low income families to help ensure that all children meet state academic standards."[2] For the most part, Title I schools are challenged academically to meet those state standards and federal achievement levels of performance. Recent data from the U.S. Department of Education indicated "that more than 56,000 public schools across the country are provided assistance to provide academic support and learning opportunities so that children can master curricula, meet state standards and reach proficiency."[3]

With knowledge of the role that Title I plays in the schools, the National Title I conference in Texas appeared to be fertile ground to discuss topics such as continuous improvement and higher performance in classrooms, schools, and districts. From our perspective, it was going to be a breakthrough moment to reach those "in the trenches." Much to our astonishment, many teachers were complacent about performance and were reluctant to discuss it. A teacher from northern Alaska stated it most appropriately, "We are Excellent! We are already Exemplary!" Others were deluded by awards such as "Blue Ribbon" recognition.

Additionally, an interesting dynamic among attendees was observed. There was a great deal of interest in specific programs or interventions targeting a narrow window of student needs without much consideration for the validity of the program or if it actually worked in "real time." Others were more interested in the programs that met a specific social and emotional student need. It was more about surviving the daily routine than the long-term impact of underachievement or reversing the overall trend of underperformance in the school or district. Most teachers felt that they were doing their best under difficult circumstances and sought solutions that provided them with some glimmer of hope.

Clearly, many within this stakeholder group are not going to initiate a school wide initiative for higher performance. They will simply close their classroom door, do what they think works, and hope that "Good Enough is really Good Enough."[4] Overall, these stakeholders are probably good teachers who nurture students but lack the school or district leadership to drive a performance/results-based platform.

To commit fully to higher performance, teachers will require assurances that the proposed changes will produce the designated results. Teacher "buy-in" requires clear and tangible benefits for their students. They must also have confidence that the results are sustainable and that there is a multi-year commitment to the plan.

Developing a sense of urgency for change will require that the leadership team provide data as to the school or district's level of functioning and make a compelling argument that through internal problem solving and planning higher performance can become a reality. It may require reflection and analysis of the disconnections that are hindering performance and developing internal solutions to address them.

Teachers are critical partners in the execution of the designed instructional program. Providing teachers with support further deepens a teacher's commitment to improvement. Besides professional development and allocating time to collaborate, this stakeholder group thrives when empowered and supported by the leadership team. When teachers begin to connect to the initiative for growth, they will drive the process for change.

Parents

Overwhelmingly, parents want the best education for their children. Not being professionals in the field of education, parents are reliant on the expertise and the judgment of educational leaders to design and provide a quality program for their children. They are dependent on those professionals to create an environment that is conducive to learning but also one in which children can acquire the skills necessary to be successful in the real world.

For the most part, parents are very content with their schools, teachers, and programs, even when those schools are deemed by state and national standards as failing. From a parent's perspective, it is always the school on the "other side of the tracks" that is failing. Rarely is there recognition that the home school needs major reform unless there are serious issues which involve security.

Moving from this "Lake Wobegon Delusion"[5] requires a planning process that involves parents.

Parents need to be convinced that the changes and direction of the district will indeed improve the learning and the futures for their children. They want to be assured that their children will be capable of reaching higher levels of achievement without frustration, embarrassment, and failure. They want assurances that their children will receive the additional help to succeed.

To alleviate concerns and rectify issues regarding the overall improvement initiatives and to clarify the district's direction, a Parent Forum was held once a month. Other smaller meetings were also held at the building level. There were some administrators who feared that these meetings would simply become a gripe session but the intention was to clarify any misconceptions before those ideas gathered momentum and to keep the performance initiative "on the rails" toward our designation.

At these meetings, it was not unusual for parents to question the validity of the new mathematics program by expressing concern over the new program's ability to maintain the current level of SAT performance, its emphasis on high level thinking skills, and the ability of students to perform on Advanced Placement tests. From the parental perspective any substantive change appeared to be a gamble but we needed them at the table to "play their cards." Others questioned whether the district was eliminating spelling and vocabulary testing. Still others discussed the daily operational aspects of the district.

Knowing that performance and achievement were our focus, all district curriculum supervisors were required to attend curriculum meetings alongside district principals and central office administrators. Often, we scheduled specific presentations for parents in curriculum areas to improve the understanding of programs and sessions were arranged in which parents could learn the material themselves. Imagine the political capital and goodwill that we developed by having access to almost every administrator at one time. It truly communicated a message that we viewed parents as partners.

Parents are powerful forces in the educational change process, but they are also subject to manipulation by those internal forces who benefit from maintaining the status quo. With this group in particular, it is essential to build a bond to demonstrate that you care about their children and their children's future. It is essential to communicate with them about instructional issues to dispel rumors and misunderstandings as well as providing assistance for children that were challenged by the new expectations.

PERFORMANCE PARADOX

At the highest levels of the federal government, the inability of state government and local districts to shift the narrative to one of performance was a concern. Dr. Arnie Duncan, former Secretary of Education, upon reflecting on school reform and change, expressed his frustration by stating that "we don't value education. We say that we do but we really don't."[6] He further supported his position by indicating that "we are not a top ten anything."[7] One such example that supports his perspective is as follows:

The urban district straddled a major interstate highway and was consistently ranked as one of the lowest performing school districts in the state. The small city which comprised the district was known for its crime, poverty, and its violence in the schools.

Waiting for the superintendent provided an opportunity to examine the array of district produced materials that were on display. The district's annual report was placed in a prominent position for all to view. The twenty-five-page annual report was printed on high grade glossy paper and appeared to be the pride of the district office if not the district in general. Upon examining it, there were photographs of students engaged in serious learning activities. All the buzz words were present in the narratives: STEM, ENGAGEMENT, ACCOUNTABILITY, ROBOTICS, TECHNOLOGY, EXCELLENCE, etc. By all accounts, they were on the move! But were they?

A deeper analysis of data indicated consistently poor academic achievement. Now this district was in jeopardy of a state takeover. In the minds of many district stakeholders, they were performing well. They were "Good Enough" given the challenges of the city and the district. There was no sense of urgency to reverse the achievement slide. Despite increased funding from the state, investment in programs, and at least on the surface, a focus on instruction, performance remained stagnant and amazingly, the stakeholders were not demanding change.

In another location, a beautiful New England city with factories that were remnants of the Industrial Revolution, the mayor with his aide reviewed our background and narrowed their inquiry to one of accountability. He noted experience regarding an accountability program and wanted to know if it impacted teacher performance. The response required a clarification which indicated that the experience referenced involved a collaborative system of accountability that included building rewards, linkage to goals and curriculum initiatives, a coordinated professional development program, and much more. Our experience focused on systemic improvement. He was looking for something that supported his campaign mantra of teacher accountability and "Pay for Performance."

Despite governing over a city with the lowest academic achievement in the New England region, the mayor did not agree to further invest in the children of his city. Specifically, the mayor stated, "I went to school with people who could not speak the language. Somehow those individuals found a place in our city. These new immigrants will also find a place."

Even though there were significant numbers in the city that vociferously expressed an opinion to begin a process of self-reflection and educational reform, the mayor rejected those ideas and was elected to two additional terms and launched a campaign for governor.

Almost 1,500 miles to the west in the Midwestern plains, a brick K–12 building of 250 students and teachers grappled with performance issues. There was no limit to the list of interconnected district and community wide issues. Again, the school and district struggled to move just one student into proficiency.

The superintendent was clear with us from the outset. I really didn't want you here. You wouldn't be here but for the board president and his wife. It was a tangled web of stakeholders vying for power and control.

Both in New England and the Midwest, the leadership readily admitted to systemic issues and a lack of coordination surrounding the problem. More importantly, they lacked the "will" to change the culture of the district. Although the issues were uncovered through internal reflection and analysis, the solutions required that local power brokers work in a coordinated manner with the district. The goal of improved performance and potentially improved futures was "Not Enough" to abandon practices that maintained the status quo.

Meanwhile in the Southeast, a large county system was struggling with student achievement. The superintendent believed that the district provided an excellent education. The school district's Director of Improvement suggested, based on their programs, that they were within striking distance of obtaining the state's "A" rating for achievement.

Was the director's description substantive or sizzle? The data revealed tremendous learning gaps among all groups of students. Teachers described the learning atmosphere as chaotic. Parents and others in the community sensed the lack of instructional focus. Board meetings were best described as dysfunctional with a focus on control and authority.

Clearly, in this case, one can "dress up" the district with programs but the disconnections were everywhere. Most stakeholders realized that the district was in real trouble and farther from the desired "A" ranking which the leadership team described as within their reach.

BREAKING DOWN PARADOXICAL BARRIERS

As clearly illustrated in several of the provided examples, building consensus among stakeholders to endorse and embrace an agenda based on performance is essential. It is a complicated journey with many moving parts. It is a journey of internal analysis and integrity which requires a moral compass.

The challenge to increasing performance in schools and districts begins with convincing educational leaders and associated stakeholders of its importance and how the outcomes will benefit not just their community but the future of the children that they serve and in the long run benefit our democracy. Even then, there are those that may resist for a variety of reasons but a non-accusatory, blameless approach for stagnation or failure often has moved stakeholders from a position of inaction to one which is willing to consider improvement.

When it is recognized that despite good intentions, expenditures, program investments and other initiatives, desired results have not been produced, the solution may be one of simply identifying the disconnections and the nuances associated with the implementation process; then stakeholders may be more willing to engage. When stakeholders recognize that the beginning point involves internal reflection and that the solutions involve building the internal capacity of the leadership team and to those delivering instruction, the resistance begins to dissipate.

The process of building a consensus among stakeholders willing to venture into the arena of higher performance is somewhat like trying to determine the best way to navigate a boat from a "fog bank." When you are surrounded by the fog all reference points disappear. The current of the water, wind direction, water depth, and sounds of other approaching boats are external pressures that may impact the decision process of how to proceed. Internal pressures of competence, skill, and leadership tug at the navigator to do something. But what?

Educational leaders find themselves in the same dilemma. They recognize that they have a problem but they either do not know what to do, lack the "will" to do it, or fear any potential fallout as the plan moves forward. Why take a chance or the risk? But clearly "floating in the fog bank" without having the skills or a plan is dangerous unto itself.

To extricate the stakeholders from the "fog of paralysis," or from seeking a quick fix, adept leaders must recognize that they need to rely on a set of synergistic guidelines and proven tools to build support. Being objective and inclusive eliminates selective fact finding and creates a culture in which real problems are collaboratively solved. It is this strategic approach that will not only unlock the gridlock but provide a sustainable path to higher performance.

In the next chapter you will find the leadership and management style along with key characteristics of performance-based leaders that establish a foundation for developing a plan that *Ignites School Performance*.

SUMMARY

- Stakeholder Paralysis is a major obstacle to higher performance.
- Multiple internal and external factors along with organizational dynamics reinforce performance stagnation.
- Building stakeholder consensus begins with an elimination of blame.
- Performance Paralysis is lifted by utilizing a leadership style and tools that build support for a higher performance agenda.

RECOMMENDATIONS

- Identify all stakeholders in the improvement process.
- Understand the factors impeding stakeholder commitment to a performance-based agenda.
- Build a collaborative, inclusive, and transparent process of engagement.
- Model a leadership style that encourages community participation.

ACTIVITIES

- Review *Appendix A* #6 and #7: Board of Directors/Administrative Retreat Framework.

Chapter 2

Performance-Focused Leadership

SYNERGISTIC AND STRATEGIC

Generally, at least on the surface, when assuming a leadership position, there is an expectation that the new leader will move the school or district forward by analyzing it and then making recommendations that have the potential to improve it. While such a change initially may appear simple, even in organizations desiring improvement or reform, embarking on such a pathway requires leaders to take stock of the complexity of the journey. It requires planning, an understanding of the dynamics of the organization, and the support of all stakeholders.

Regardless of how a leader approaches the challenge of improvement and in particular, in setting a bar of high expectations and higher performance, the leader needs to adopt an approach that is both synergistic and strategic. Adept leaders are synergistic from the perspective of enjoining all stakeholders in the mission and vision of the organization while at the same time being strategic in the planning and execution process. A blending of both leadership approaches, which is necessary for igniting performance, is what this author has defined as *"synertegic"* leadership.

"Synergistic leadership is not focused on the leader but rather on getting teams to align, to create together and to merge those pieces in an organizational symphony."[1] It is essentially about aligning the energy of the organization. "The synergist brings together a primary focus on what is best for the enterprise as a whole, and they choreograph and harmonize a team or group interactions to produce high quality decisions."[2] The Blue Angels, the epitome of excellence and performance, extend the concept of synergy to include the elements such as values, team, communication, respect, and attitude in striving for perfection.

With the new rules of power and influence relying less on traditional command and control models, strategic leadership is focused more on knowing the essential insights, frameworks, and tools of leverage to influence others. It is essentially not only knowing how to execute a plan for improvement and to develop a consensus among stakeholders to move in a certain direction but to sustain the initiative until the school or district reaches higher performance levels.

When the forces of synergy and strategy are combined, the outcomes can produce dramatic results. Before their 2018 Super Bowl victory, Doug Pederson, coach of the Philadelphia Eagles, prophetically stated that "individuals make a difference but it takes a team to make a miracle." In another prophetic statement, a lineman, realizing the importance of team and the synergy needed to win stated that "WE, all we got. WE, all we need." With minutes remaining in the game, Nick Foles, the Eagles Quarterback, assessed the defense and called a play which caught the Patriots off guard. It was an unexpected play but strategic at this point in the game. It was the classic combination of synergy and strategy.

The dynamics of school districts in contemporary America is extremely complex with an array of socioeconomic demographics layered with generational expectations and beliefs regarding the schools. All of those factors contribute to stakeholder perspectives on a multitude of school district issues. Often, there is a convergence of those perspectives when school board meetings are held to discuss district improvement, instructional change, or the budget. In those situations, an effective leader, one who is both synergistic and strategic, is needed. Learning the importance of both leadership skills was the result of one such meeting.

It appeared simple enough. The budget included a very basic and minimal increase. We did a great job of eliminating unproductive programs and reallocating resources to those areas in need of improvement. The board subcommittee meetings were held without much public reaction. Tonight's meeting was the "first reading or first review" of the budget with the Board of Directors at one of its regular meetings. It was also the first budget meeting with the new superintendent at the helm. Anticipating the nuances associated with the budget, various community members from our subcommittees were invited to attend the meeting.

As the residents began to take their seats for the meeting, it was clear that members of a district tax reform group began to enter the room. In the past, tax reform groups had grown accustomed to administrators who purchased instructional programs which appeared on the surface capable of producing genuine outcomes but "at the end of the day" these programs provided no real tangible results. This group, due to their political affiliation and political connections, had the leverage to "sideline" any initiative. The meeting could go "sideways" as a result of external pressure. Our initial planning with stakeholders in the development of a long-range performance improvement plan might go to the wayside as part of a board compromise or political appeasement. In this particular situation, the board and the administration reached a defining moment in its history, one that would impact the district's achievement forever.

During the discussion phase of the meeting, members of the tax group challenged budget expenditures as well as the cost of the performance initiative known as "Reaching Above and Beyond." Immediately, the district's stakeholders defended the initiative. Board members, parents, principals, and teachers discussed the importance of improving the district's performance and how this initiative could positively impact the future of the children in the district. Clearly, we had built a consensus among our stakeholders and it was strategic to invite them to attend the budget adoption hearings. After all, they were our partners in formulating a process to improve performance. The budget passed unanimously.

Without our stakeholder partners and the foresight of how to utilize them in the adoption process, the budget, which was now instructionally focused, would have failed in a dramatic fashion. Having an understanding of what was necessary to finish such an adoption and the nuances associated with it are part of a skill set necessary to lead a performance initiative. Other characteristics of a performance-based or "synertegic" leader include the following:

- Visionary
- Reflective
- Analytical
- Instructionally Focused
- Non-Adversarial
- Motivational
- Methodical

Some might argue that leadership is situational and that the circumstances of the time and place demand a particular type of leader but as far as the performance aspect of leadership is concerned, an array of higher administrative skills is necessary to produce performance-based outcomes.

In some very tough educational settings, few would argue that there are a number of non-negotiable policies and regulations. Generally, these management issues involve discipline and other operational issues which require a very direct leadership style. Others such as Bolman and Deal suggest that leaders are "wizards and warriors" who can "move in and out" of roles, even if they are more comfortable with one or the other.[3]

Wizards, despite the odds, are able to "pull a rabbit out of a hat" through a combination of technical skill and persuasion. Warriors, on the other hand, tend to take the "bull by the horns," grind it out by sheer will and direct influence. Whether "wizard" or "warrior," the leader will enter an arena laden with obstacles, dynamics, traditions, and subcultures, which demand both skill and savvy. They have a knowledge base of how to overcome these challenges and how to generate high performance outcomes. Adept leaders possess substance, sizzle, and technical ability with an instinct of when to utilize each separately or together.

Given the characteristics embodied in a "synertegic" leader, the district will proceed along a journey to higher performance unlike those who have ventured into this arena without the proper skill set, experience, or knowledge base. It will be a journey without major turmoil, one that utilizes the existing resources and talent. It will ignite real results. It will be a journey in which all stakeholders celebrate its success because it was inclusive and collaborative but more importantly because it ignited the potential of ALL children.

SUMMARY

- Improving the performance of a school or district is a complex undertaking that requires an understanding of its organizational dynamics.
- Leaders who are focused on performance are both synergistic and strategic.
- Combining synergy and strategy is known as "synertegic" leadership.
- Several performance characteristics comprise a performance-based leadership model.
- Performance-based leadership involves higher level administrative skills.
- Skilled and savvy leaders are not one dimensional.

RECOMMENDATIONS

- Conduct numerous meetings with all stakeholders of the district to understand their issues and concerns.
- Understand the history of the district, the "How" and the "Why" of its current state and level of functioning.
- Function both in a synergistic and strategic manner.
- Adopt all characteristics of a "synertegic" leader.
- Recognize that performance-based leadership can be situational, but it is always focused on instructional outcomes.

ACTIVITIES

- Complete *Appendix B* #1: "Wizard or Warrior."
- Complete *Appendix B* #4: Synergistic or Strategic.

Chapter 3

Principles of Performance

FIVE GUIDING PRINCIPLES

"Child First Focus"

If you were to interview board members, central office administrators, and principals regarding the focus of a school-based organization, most would respond that it exists to support the children. Seems like a very reasonable response, but if one were to continue this inquiry by further asking others such as teachers, parents, and community members, the responses may vary to include statements like: politics, jobs, power, tax control, and so forth. The latter statements might be symptomatic of disconnections in implementing the organization's focus, vision, mission.

Most organizations have lofty mission statements such as "to prepare children for the future," or "to create life-long learners." Only with an in-depth examination of the district's strategic plan and affiliated improvement plans associated with its practices, policies, procedures, resource allocation, and execution plans can one truly determine if those mission statements are real or superfluous. Experience has also proven that stakeholder statements which question the focus of a district are minimally "red flags" that indicate the existence of major issues.

For schools and districts to reach high levels of performance, a "Child First Focus" is the fundamental platform from which to launch a performance agenda. Every aspect of the organization must be measured through this lens, and every member of the organization must embrace this principle. Whether it involves the adoption of a budget at a board meeting or simply repairing a broken window, there should always be a connection as to how the expenditure, the task, the initiative, or activity benefits the child.

As a new superintendent, it appeared to be a good idea to discuss our new operational principles with the board. When reviewing the "Child First Focus," a board member, who was the former president and one with a reputation of being cantankerous, called us out. Frankly, it shocked us that anyone would challenge this concept particularly at a public meeting but his rationale made perfect sense. He explained that "in the past they were always told that purchasing this program, that program or adopting an initiative always was good for the child or student. How do we know that this focus is any different?" It was a question that made us pause for a second or two but not much longer. Too much of a delay in responding would create a level of uncertainty.

It was then explained to him that there were other levels of scrutiny that would be embedded into an adoption process that would sharpen our focus. It was further explained that we always include research and data in the review process and eventually, accountability before making a recommendation.

The leadership team was not sure if this was a test or a quiz but they left the room with a better understanding of how we were going to operate in the future. The dialogue also suggested that there was renewed confidence in the team to finally deliver a program that makes the student the real priority.

Systemic

While some areas of a school or district may require immediate or short-term attention, a performance-based agenda's larger focus is the systemic improvement of the organization and all of its component parts. If the whole is the sum of its parts, then logically, a school-based organization should examine all of its components that contribute to performance. There was recognition of the interdependence of instructional components, and how each contributed to the school or district's success.

In an organization as complex as a school district, there are a myriad of possible "disconnections" that may contribute to its underperformance. To assure high performance outcomes, it is suggested that leaders develop a K–12 improvement plan which addresses all organizational levels, all grades, all subject areas, and all departments. It is important to communicate that each member of the organization is tied to the success of the plan.

Too often, stakeholders dismiss systemic improvement by referencing the existing school or district's strategic plan but the major difference between strategic and systemic plans is one of targeted performance. The systemic nature of a performance agenda requires the identification of the disconnections within the organization's key elements and further analyzes its policies and procedures.

Performance improvement plans provide specifics as to how to remediate the disconnections, develop a timeline and assign responsibility to complete them. These plans are actionable and flexible. If designed properly, they can meet mandates and requirements driven by state and federal governments.

The major challenge with systemic improvement is that all stakeholders and all educational leaders want the identified issues addressed immediately across all organizational levels. It is understandable because educational leaders and parents want the best program for their children. Compounding the challenge is that they want it now, not later.

We were underperforming! We were near the bottom of the county in achievement and our parents understood the future impact of such underperformance. Our children's access to college, training programs, and other opportunities would be limited.

Our plan was to sequence our improvement efforts by organizational level. The sequence was K-3, followed by the intermediate grades (4,5,6), then the middle school, and finally efforts at the high school. Everyone wanted it done tomorrow but it was going to take time. At a parent forum, a parent challenged the timeline by explaining that her children at the high school were running out of time.

The dilemma was real and one that tugged at your heart. Having children, it was easy to empathize with her but with limited resources, we had to balance realistic growth against empathy and at the same time we had to find meaningful "stop gap" measures to alleviate her concerns.

While we aggressively implemented reform at the K-3 level, the foundation for future change was also being established at other grade levels. Methodological reforms were integrated into all strands of the curriculum as a culture of continuous improvement began "to take root" and flourish.

Strategically, when the reforms were implemented at the lower grade levels of the organization, we projected that any future resistance to change, particularly at the secondary level, would eventually dissipate. Parents and students would have tangible evidence of positive growth and demand a similar shift in the culture of teaching and learning at all levels.

Upon reviewing our systemic improvement plan, an expert in the field informed us that it would take 7 years. We did it in 5, and some 18 years later this culture of improvement continues to flourish. Student achievement continually ranks among the highest in the state.

Fundamentally, attempting to make changes across all organizational levels at one time is the biggest mistake that a district can make. Going too fast can result in peripheral issues that diffuse and distract from the improvement efforts. Trying to do too much at one time contributes to miscommunication and poor implementation. For success to take hold, implementation plans must be structured, purposeful, involve training, and evolve in a logical manner from a strong foundation of principles and guidelines.

Professional development and building the internal capacity of the organization is an essential component to systemic and substantive growth. Not spending the time to train and equip the facility and staff with the essential skills for successful program implementation can be disastrous. A teacher in a neighboring school district illustrated the problem of "going too fast, too soon."

A distraught, veteran teacher explained how the superintendent and the board adopted a new reading program over the summer. The adoption took place without committee formation or teacher input. She said, "It just happened over the summer." She returned to school and new books were in the room. We had no professional development and no understanding of the program.

We were told that we were teachers and that we would "figure it out." They never did "figure it out." Two years and some $300,000 later, the program was dropped.

Other than having secured the funding, it wasn't clear why the district opted to implement a district wide program in such a limited time frame. This reading program was doomed from the outset. The program not only failed, it imploded without the necessary "buy-in." Not only did it waste resources, but it was a lost opportunity. Its failure further highlighted disconnections related to trust and potentially alienated stakeholders from investing in the future of the district.

Successful systemic implementation is strategic, synergistic, and incremental.

Analytical

From its inception, a performance-based agenda must integrate analytical components into its fabric for improvement. In creating a sense of urgency among stakeholders that the "status quo" is no longer acceptable, leaders must be skillful in utilizing data that identifies the disconnections which are impeding performance as well as being adept in determining the causation of those deficiencies.

Effectively analyzing the data and communicating the underlying issues that are obstructing student achievement in a manner that is logical and understandable assists in building a consensus to "go in another direction." At the same time, providing data regarding specific issues and providing research-based solutions assist in building a "critical mass" of stakeholders willing to risk departure from the status quo.

Having an analytical framework and associated tools that provide direction and objectivity will assist the leadership team in maintaining its focus on the elements that will improve performance. While research commonly cites frameworks such as Baldridge,[1] Lezotte's Correlates,[2] or other such models for improvement, personal experience in a variety of settings has shown that a focus on the following four specific elements have ignited both performance and creativity in an organization:

- Alignment
- Attitude and Atmosphere
- Accountability
- Adept Leadership

Recognizing the importance of how each of these elements contributes to the overall effectiveness of the organization is essential, but most importantly, it is an understanding of the interrelationship of each element to one another that fundamentally changes the organization. Rather than being distinct and separate entities, each element overlays and interacts with the other elements. A disconnection in any one element has the potential to impact the quality of the organization's outcomes. Each element must fit the organization perfectly for it to function in a manner that meets the organization's objectives, goals, and outcomes.

An analytical framework acts as a reference point to decision makers, leaders, and stakeholders in developing performance improvement plans, considering the effectiveness of current programs and the adoption of new initiatives. The framework keeps everyone on the same page by acting as a guide in providing direction and even resolving internal disputes. The elements in the framework become non-negotiable in a performance-based agenda.

A debate was raging at one of our middle schools after submitting its improvement plan for the year. The parameters for growth were clearly communicated to each building. Instructional supervisors assisted with the dissection of the data and areas which needed to be addressed but the improvement team was empowered to develop a plan to address those deficiencies in a way that was unique to their building. Unfortunately, everyone that reviewed the building plan at the central office was not satisfied with it.

The principal contacted the superintendent's office and requested assistance in resolving the issue. Previously, the supervisors tried to resolve it. The principal tried to work the magic of personal persuasion without resolution. Given the impasse, a meeting with the team was scheduled.

The oversized table in the small conference room at the middle school always created a formal climate to what, in this case, was supposed to be an informal discussion. In the room the eight members of the improvement team appeared angry. The team was heavily laden with strong union leaders.

Our goal was to diffuse the situation without compromising the district's framework for improvement. Team members sat erectly in their chairs, arms crossed and tightly holding them against their chests.

Immediately, building team members indicated that they were empowered to develop a plan. The problem from our perspective was that the plan held everyone else accountable for its implementation and its results. In other words, central office personnel were assigned to implement the middle school plan and were also responsible for its outcomes.

In resolving the issue, the team was reminded that ownership of the plan is correlated to the plan's success. Empowerment could only occur if members owned the implementation and the targeted outcomes. Assigning the critical elements of alignment and accountability to central office personnel mitigated the concept of empowerment and ownership. The argument held and the team agreed. Was luck a factor, a persuasive argument or the framework, that convinced them to "play ball"? Most of those involved believed that it was the framework and the adherence to the interrelated elements of alignment, accountability, and atmosphere.

Instructional

For a performance-based improvement plan to reach its targeted outcomes, it clearly must address deficiencies in the area of teaching and learning. This sounds obvious, but having examined a number of performance plans, schools, and districts can get sidetracked in writing plans that include items that are not directly related to instruction. Too often, the administration is pressured by peripheral stakeholders, legislators, or other groups to implement an initiative that has little or no bearing on performance or real academic achievement. Unfortunately, these initiatives are emotionally laden items with no research to support them.

Gimmicks, "quick fixes," and "silver bullet" solutions can gain momentum because they promise a big gain in achievement with virtually little effort. These fixes were often contemptuously known as "this year's new thing." The genesis of these programs evolves from a news story, an article, a conference, or a passionate stakeholder, but often these programs lack the proven instructional research to improve performance.

Even when one examines research-based programs in a school or district that is underperforming, the answer for its performance should begin with an examination of the nuances in the implementation process, which is inherent in any program. The answer does not involve purchasing another program or developing a gimmick that artificially projects an image of improved performance.

We were experiencing a real problem with our foreign language program. After consecutive years in the program, few students were fluent in the language of their choice. At a conference, like most professionals, our efforts in the exhibit hall focused on those companies that could remedy our problem. One company, affiliated with a pedigree university, indicated that their technology program was the solution. When the representative could not guarantee that our students would be linguistically fluent after exposure to their program, it was obvious to us that we needed our faculty to tackle the problem and own it.

Upon returning from the conference, a committee of teachers was formed to examine the areas of the curriculum that were problematic and develop several solutions to them. The answer to our issue was internally resolved. This instructional partnership between administrators, teachers, and parents became the "starting line" in resolving teaching and learning issues. The faculty appreciated the trust demonstrated by the administration in having faith in their ability to resolve this instructional issue. More importantly, the rate of fluency increased dramatically in the years that followed.

For a plan to be successful, stakeholders must examine the curriculum in an in-depth manner, focus on how to improve its delivery and how to monitor it. Heidi Hayes Jacobs suggested developing a curriculum map[3] and a list of "Essential Questions" as a baseline for student mastery.[4] When the content, standards, expectations, and delivery become transparent versus a secret formula for a select few to discover in a random trial-and-error manner, all children will succeed.

Other models for instructional analysis abound. Grant Wiggins and Jay McTighe's "Understanding by Design,"[5] examines curriculum, planning, assessments, and programming. Marzano's "Using Common Core Standards"[6] or Jeff Colosimo's "EduPlanet21"[7] framework aligns learning goals, assessments, and strategies through a technology platform. Regardless of the model, it is the quality of the content in the curriculum and how it is delivered that ultimately counts.

A rigorous instructional analysis in all areas of the curriculum must be the core of any plan designed to ignite instruction. The quality of the analysis will dictate the quality of program. The goal of instructional analysis is to "guarantee a viable curriculum which ensures all students an equal opportunity to learn."[8]

To fulfill the promise of success for every student, each student must have access to the same content. The content must always be relevant, rigorous, and of the highest quality. It is only when these parameters are in place that higher performance can be reached.

Measurable

When it comes to a performance-based agenda for improvement, the old adage, "if it gets measured, it will get done," rings true today. The bigger question is one of what exactly is being measured. In an attempt to improve performance, superintendents, principals, and supervisors may actually measure items that have little or no significant impact on instruction. They generate meaningless data or even worse, interpret data in a manner that takes the school or district "down an alley" that's "a dead end."

In *Measure What Matters*, John Doerr "highlights the importance of measuring very specific objectives and goals with verifiable and tangible results."[9] In fact, "a two-year Deloitte study found no single factor has more impact than clearly defined goals that are written and shared freely."[10]

Even when goals are clearly defined and transparent, understanding the key elements for higher performance (Alignment, Atmosphere/Attitude, Accountability, and Leadership) and integrating those elements into a framework for improvement is critical. Equally important is connecting the skills of teaching and learning to those elements while measuring them in a numerical and coherent manner.

For real growth to occur, a school or district cannot just "cling to the past and only rely on what has worked"[11] but rather seek to utilize research and experiment. With knowledge from our collective experiences we can "pry open the door" to new levels of achievement. At every stage of implementation, the objectives, goals, benchmarks, and indicators must be measured in a definitive manner. It is this rigorous process that "drives clarity, accountability, and the uninhabited pursuit of greatness."[12]

THE POWER OF PERFORMANCE PRINCIPLES

With a set of performance principles "in place" to guide a leader in building a culture of higher performance, there is a greater likelihood that the instructional environment will mirror the vision and mission of an organization which seeks to build its internal capacity along with increasing the achievement levels of those that it serves. If adopted by the administrative team, these principles will assist leaders and stakeholders in the decision-making process that shapes the policies, procedures, and plans to improve performance. A dialogue of performance will permeate throughout the district in everything the district does.

Without a defined set of performance principles, almost every aspect of the organization becomes prone to inconsistency, to random outcomes, and even chaos.

As a member of an "inner city" administrative team, it felt like we are always reacting to everything, whether it was a disciplinary situation that required immediate attention or a decree from the central office for implementation. Ad hoc committees were continually formed and disbanded. After each faculty meeting it always seemed like there was another initiative that required immediate implementation for the sake of meeting an arbitrary timeline or for someone with "political clout."

The combination of state and local reforms along with other pressures exerted on the school left it rudderless and functioning in a survival mode. Faculty and staff questioned the logic of decisions, procedures, and policies while others questioned the values and beliefs of the organization. Everyone was on their own to simply "keep the lid on the place." No one had a sense of where we were going other than to help children learn and maybe make a difference along the way.

Now consider what happens when there is a systematic decision-making process which incorporates key performance principles into the process, and these principles are also embedded in the organizational culture. From the boardroom to classroom, everyone appears on the same page. All the components of the organization are synchronized to deliver a program that focuses on instructional outcomes.

In another organization, the culture embraced principles of performance. Its focus and connectedness are illustrated below:

Whether it was a board member, principal, teacher or parent, inquiries always focused on how a program, expenditure, or initiative would benefit the students. It was a "line in the sand." While most leaders might respond by providing a rationale that connects to helping students, what made us different were the questions and the answers associated with research, data, sustainability, alignment, accountability, and so forth.

It was apparent that there was a strong instructional focus but more importantly, that focus was shared by all of its stakeholders. There was an interconnectedness of all the organizational components to the principles that drove a performance agenda. There was a thorough analysis and review process that eliminated distractions that often find a way to derail such an agenda.

As these illustrations demonstrate, these principles are the "secret sauce" in a recipe that when blended synergistically and executed strategically delivers huge performance dividends.

SUMMARY

- The principles of performance provide a guideline in developing a performance-based agenda for improvement in a school or district.

- These principles will drive a mindset that is analytical, research-based, and instructional throughout plan development and implementation.
- A framework that incorporates the elements of Alignment, Atmosphere/Attitude, Accountability, and Adept Leadership and the interconnection of each element will identify disconnections related to an organization's objectives, goals, and outcomes.
- Maintain an instructional focus in every aspect of the plan.
- All results must be measurable and verifiable.
- Adherence to the principles will assist in creating a focus that is coherent and embedded in the culture of the school or district.
- Performance improvement is systemic but implemented incrementally.

RECOMMENDATIONS

- Build or adopt a framework that incorporates the principles of performance into the decision making and improvement process of the school or district.
- Facilitate a "Child First" philosophy that permeates throughout the organization.
- Develop a plan for incremental implementation.
- Create a "litmus" test for the analysis of components included in a performance-based plan for improvement.
- Focus on instruction and eliminate peripheral distractions.
- Develop specific criteria for determining success or failure.

ACTIVITIES

- Complete *Appendix B #5*: Guiding Principles.

Part II

IGNITING THE FIRE

"If you don't know where you are going, you might not get there."
—Yogi Berra

In this section of *Igniting School Performance*, you will be provided with the specific steps, processes, procedures, and tools that may be utilized in building a high performance-based organization. From the process of identifying talent and the leadership skills that are required to the actual steps which are necessary to mobilize all stakeholders in building a performance agenda, leaders will be provided with the "signage" and a road map to transition a school or district to one that will produce high performance outcomes.

Chapter 4

Building Performance Chemistry

Creating a team that can effectively implement a performance-based achievement plan for improvement is fundamental for its ultimate success. Without a cohesive team at all levels of the organization that "buy-in" to the components of the plan, it will needlessly stumble and progress will grind to a halt. The process of building a performance-oriented team is a multi-dimensional process involving recruitment, hiring, and team building. Getting everyone in the "right seats of the bus" and driving it in the right direction is clearly the function of strategic and synergistic leadership that blends the efforts of all stakeholders in a synchronistic manner.

RECRUITMENT AND HIRING PROCESS

We have all been there at some point in the interview process. The applications have been reviewed with great scrutiny, the job description was critiqued, the interview questions were completed, the rubrics were tabulated but yet your gut isn't quite sure if the finalist is truly the best candidate. "Only time will tell" if the selected individual will perform as expected.

You squirm a little in your chair as you offer the candidate the job because you know, as a leader, that this interview may be your only chance to hire the right person for this position. Hopefully, they will be a contributor and not a detractor.

The recruitment and hiring process is one of the most essential functions that a leader can perform and at the same time it is one of the most difficult of tasks to effectively conduct. There are many factors to consider including the nature of the candidate's characteristics, skills, and potential. Over the years, researchers have tried to provide a more objective and scientific approach that assists leaders in structuring interviews in a more effective manner. The questions are usually structured in a manner to include areas such as:

- Background
- Subject Competence and Grade Level Experience
- Teacher Technique
- Philosophy
- Evaluation of Student Performance
- Classroom Organization/Planning
- Control and Management
- Professional Activities/Knowledge

Other systems such as the "Teacher Perceiver"[1] attempt to identify those individuals that demonstrate a commitment to a student's social, emotional, and academic well-being. Some of these traits include empathy, rapport with students, listening skills, activation (ability to stimulate student thinking), focus, and objectivity. Still other researchers have encouraged the utilization of rubrics in creating a framework for the consistency in the rating of candidates.

While the increased structuring of the interview process makes for an efficient use of time, leaders need to build some flexibility into the developed structures which allow the interview committee an opportunity to explore and discover who the "real candidate" might be. By doing their research, candidates can easily provide the committee with the current "buzz words" to "game the process."

To minimize "gaming the system," the committee should provide the candidate with a scenario which enables the committee to explore a candidate's thinking and inherent beliefs. It also allows the committee to determine the extent of the candidate's ability to problem solve and to handle stress. Getting to the core of what comprises a candidate's belief system is often revealed in informal dialogue when the candidate is less guarded.

As the interview proceeded regarding a candidate for a mathematics position at the high school, it was evident that they were knowledgeable, poised, and intelligent. He was a graduate of the school district and a highly regarded local college. He was the perfect candidate but yet something was nagging at those in the room. It was hard to read his emotional quotient. Specifically, what was in his "soul?" What were his real beliefs about teaching and learning?

Deviating from the structured format, he was asked to describe his model teacher. In other words, he was asked to select a previous teacher from whom he might model his instruction. He responded with the name of a teacher, who unbeknownst to the candidate was an individual that was periodically on intervention.

The identified teacher was bright, intelligent, and knew his subject matter but continually had issues with student relationships. On too many occasions, this teacher was sarcastic and embarrassed students with his snide remarks. All too often the principal was putting out unnecessary fires in his classroom. Consequently, based on the candidate's response, we decided to pursue another candidate. Whether fair or not, we were not going to take a chance of repeating a hiring misstep.

Most recently, leaders have increasingly applied technology or technology-driven programs to screen applications which are based on selected parameters. Some leaders have utilized other devices to record the interview and the exact responses of the candidates. Like most technology initiatives in education, if utilized properly, the school or district can experience efficiencies regarding time, effort, and accuracy.

Researcher Donald Merle Chalker acknowledged the need to refine technology in the interview process.[2] If utilized poorly, it may hinder the school or district's real objective of identifying real talent. It may limit the talent pool and depersonalize the process. One such situation was brought to my attention.

Like many school districts we were always interested in identifying and hiring the "best and the brightest" available in the talent pool. Our high school principal was of the belief that the "best and the brightest" could be found in the most selective colleges and universities in the region. Having given our principals and the search committees a great deal of latitude in the hiring process, the principal and committee delineated the parameters through the use of a search program to only include graduates from these select colleges and universities.

As programmed, the computer identified individuals from elite colleges and several of those individuals were hired. Initially, the board was impressed that our district could attract such talent. Kudos poured in from the community regarding the optics of hiring such achievers. It appeared that they were going to take teaching and learning to the next level.

Unfortunately, over the course of the year, each person struggled in the classroom. Even with significant assistance and support, they just could not get comfortable with the rigors of teaching.

For us it was a failed experiment because the design parameters were flawed from the outset. Despite good intentions, the committee missed something. Was it the lack of preparation at the college level? Were they really "cut out" to teach or did they simply not understand the commitment that teaching requires?

The parameters were expanded in the replacement process and the positions were filled with teachers from less selective colleges. These selections eventually flourished in the classroom. The replacements understood the demands of the position, the work ethic that it required, and the importance of designing instruction to meet the needs of all children. We learned to dig and find that "diamond in the rough."

In another section of the county, two administrators were tasked with hiring a new teacher. Both highly competent administrators conducted the requisite due diligence of the application review process and developed questions that were specifically designed for the vacancy. From a technical perspective, it appeared to be an effective design that would yield the perfect candidate but in this case the misuse of technology seemed to depersonalize the process.

The interview apparently began with the cursory introductions and was followed by a barrage of questions. Each response was rapidly recorded on a laptop for accuracy by both administrators. In an effort to maintain a verbatim account of the interview, neither administrator had an opportunity to make significant eye contact with the candidate or was afforded the time to examine the interviewee's demeanor.

Little time was allocated to make an emotional connection with the candidate and to explore the qualities that are necessary when building a team which is focused on performance and internal chemistry. Given the narrow focus of the interview team, it was no surprise that the selected candidate struggled with interpersonal relationships.

STRATEGIC SELECTION OF PERSONNEL

In order to become a high performing school or district, a leader must build a culture of achievement. The selection of both new personnel and those being considered for a leadership role is an opportunity for a leader to shape the current and future of the school or district.

When a leader utilizes a process that clearly addresses the needs of the organization by targeting those with specific skill sets, the process becomes strategic. When a leader utilizes a team approach in filling the position, the process is synergistic because it builds a culture of inclusion and empowerment. It is only when the leader combines strategy with synergy through collaboratively developed criteria that the selection process becomes effective.

How a leader defines the selection criteria will eventually either enhance or hinder the organization's goal of improved performance. Ultimately, it will determine the type of person that will fill the position. Selecting candidates with the mindset, personality, ability, and other inherent intangibles that blend effectively with those of the existing team are important criteria for consideration.

Candidates may meet the base criteria of certification, GPA, content expertise, and recommendations, but it is the following attributes that must also be embedded into the selection process to reveal individuals capable of succeeding in a team environment with a focus on performance.

ATTRIBUTES FOR SUCCESS

Attitude

How often have you heard someone say: I don't like their attitude! Unfortunately, you may have heard such a statement on more than one occasion. Within that statement is an understanding that the individual might be termed difficult, uncooperative, or not a team player depending on its context. There are also those that can exhibit this behavior in a harmful passive aggressive manner while others exhibit it in more overt ways.

As a young "20 something" new teacher assigned to an "inner city" school, the challenge of organizing a classroom, designing lessons and activities for group of students not accustomed to structure was daunting. Layered on this challenge was a schedule that required floating to three different rooms throughout the day. Without a home base, it was necessary to arrive early and go to each of the four rooms to list the daily instructional directions on a side blackboard.

With permission from the room's teacher who was a member of our grade level team, key information and content was displayed for the class which occupied the room for only one period. The goal was to get the students working in the room before the teacher's arrival and to minimize the time of writing on the blackboard while there, particularly when the teacher's back was turned to the class. Before departing each room, bold capitalized letters alerted the home teacher to DO NOT ERASE!

Upon returning later in the day, all the information was erased. The teacher simply said that they needed the space although there was nothing written there. It was discouraging but you learned quickly to navigate around the obstacles.

It was also an indication that this person was not a team player and without everyone working together we would competitively toil in our own silos without the collaboration required for success. It also provided several lessons about resilience.

Don't wallow in the issue but rather solve it and move on. Find an approach to work around it so tomorrow will be better.

In an atmosphere of continuous improvement, it is essential to have individuals that are extremely positive, inclusive, collaborative, and respectful of the role that each member of the organization plays, regardless of level or job description. It is simply an implied understanding that "we are all in this together." We either work together or fail.

Meeting the school or district's goal of higher performance is increasingly difficult without a team effort. When everyone is united in purpose, the outcome is always better. Admiral Hyman G. Rickover stated that "plans and programs don't get things done. It takes people."[3]

Rarely, do new teachers or administrators initially know everything that is needed to teach or lead, let alone being masters in the "art of teaching and learning." Most experienced educators acknowledge that it was only after several years that "it all started to come together" in the form of the components that made them more effective teachers and administrators. For it to "come together," they needed the requisite attitude that prized continuous learning and yearned for collaboration. They had to acknowledge that they were really "still a work in progress." Otherwise, it is far too easy to retreat to practices that may be comfortable for them but not really very effective.

The Blue Angels, the premier U.S. Navy's aviation team, recognizes the importance of building synergy through an attitude that is reflected in team planning, learning, collaboration, and mutual respect. It is summarized in the statement: ATTITUDE = ALTITUDE![4]

Character

If there is no substitute for a good Attitude then there is also no substitute for the character traits embodied within a positive attitude. These traits are often the intangibles that are difficult to ascertain in an interview process but are clearly demonstrated in their practice, particularly in a climate of change, reform, and continuous improvement.

Striving to become a high performing organization can create internal tension as expectations increase, allocations are adjusted, and methodological approaches are revised. All of these adjustments can impact relationships, alliances, and the internal dynamics when a school or district shifts its focus to one of performance.

Even when initiatives are implemented in an inclusive and collaborative manner, internal factions may react to manipulate others in order to support the status quo or past practices. When schools or districts are in the midst of a reform, the character of those dedicated to a "Child First" and performance-based agenda becomes very evident.

"Child First" advocates are often the individuals willing to speak openly, without fear of reprisal or being ostracized, on behalf of the initiative. These individuals are genuine collaborators and team players who place the interest of the child before those with adult-focused agendas. Generally, they are resilient and persevere through difficult situations.

During a hurricane we were inundated with 20 inches of rain within a several hours. Even though the school was a very safe venue, it was decided that the school would be dismissed early as the intensity of the storm increased. Numerous staff members stayed as long as possible to make sure that each and every student reached home safely and helped to secure the facility before leaving for their homes. It was a voluntary act and a choice that each person made, based on their individual circumstances.

Rather than leave immediately with the students, many stayed behind to help. It demonstrated that intangible element of dedication and commitment, to getting the job done, to completing the mission. No one inquired about contractual obligations.

Many returned to flooded basements and leaky roofs but placed our mission before personal concerns. The child entrusted to us came first.

To explore candidate traits such as work ethic, dedication, commitment, and integrity, scenarios designed to "flesh out" beliefs, values, and principles can be utilized. It is clearly better to explore these areas at the time of the interview rather than finding out later that the candidate doesn't possess them.

A selection process that is void of defined character traits can result in significant damage to the culture of the organization over a number of years. In a pressurized performance-based environment, character is often tested when student results are correlated to outcomes. The pressure to meet certain goals can result in the manipulation of data.

In Philadelphia and other large city systems such as Atlanta, assessment procedures and protocols were compromised by both teachers and administrators.[5] In another part of the country, the Florida Department of Education, when analyzing district data, noticed a 700 percent increase in graduation rates in one district and immediately suspected an intentional manipulation of the data.[6] Such unethical behavior can derail efforts to utilize data, undermine assessment practices, and lead others to question the validity of improvement efforts.

Selecting individuals for key roles without the requisite attitude and character traits may also produce team members that impede progress. Passive aggressive behavior or undermining activities can "submarine" an initiative internally. It is akin to a hidden cancer that slowly festers and eventually contaminates the climate through negativity and obstructive behavior.

Verifiable Skills

It is also a "given" that a candidate should be knowledgeable and competent in the area of one's certification, but often it is worth verifying that information in a very practical manner.

Most interviews focus on verbal responses to a series of questions which rightfully examine an individual's "presence" and communication skills. Often overlooked are a candidate's written skills and even their content knowledge.

More often than not, most interviewers assume that it is unnecessary to verify skills since the candidate graduated from college or has received an advanced degree. While that assumption is a fairly safe one in most hiring scenarios, going beyond the normal hiring protocol may be necessary when filling a vacant position that requires the hiring of an individual with technical skill or an understanding of complex subject matter.

As principal, it was shocking to observe internal candidates seeking to move from the middle level to the high school struggling with a simple content competency test.

All of the teachers were respected members of the teaching community. They were seeking to apply for a physics vacancy. All were certified in science but physics is a unique content area. With few state-wide graduates with a certification in physics, an internal candidate appeared the best approach to fill the vacancy but one's instincts indicated that it was worth verifying their content knowledge.

Each applicant was given a problem from a high school physics text to solve. It was designed by the Science Department Chair. Of the five internal candidates, only one could solve the problem. How could we expect the candidates to teach the content if they could not solve a routine physics word problem? On other occasions written assignments exposed poor writing, spelling, and critical thinking skills.

Whether the skills involve communication, content knowledge, writing or critical thinking, each candidate should be able to demonstrate them in a tangible manner. Taking a moment to verify these skills will strengthen the selection process and yield a finalist who is capable of building the internal capacity of the organization.

Platform of Success

A final and often overlooked criterion is the degree to which the candidate has been exposed to progressive ideas, methodology, and reform. In other words, what was the quality of their teaching or administrative experience? What were their challenges and how did they overcome them? Were they ever exposed to students that were different from them and how were they able to relate to them? Were they willing "to step outside their comfort zone?"

New teachers and administrators often emulate the behavior to which they have been exposed so it became a threshold from which to begin our discovery about the candidate. With that parameter in place, we sought individuals that could extend themselves beyond that threshold.

We wanted to pursue individuals that were curious. We sought new staff members who were exposed to new ideas, approaches, programs, and were willing to experiment and learn.

By screening for individuals with this type of background, we theorized that it would infuse the organization with new ideas. It was hoped that they would continually revitalize us. To some degree when we got it right, we were "pressing our refresh button."

ORGANIZATIONAL CHEMISTRY

Ask the coach of any winning team the reason for their success and most will reply that it is the chemistry of the group. It is how they interact and complement the skill set of their teammates.

Great coaches understand that you can recruit the best players in the nation, but it is the chemistry among those players that is the formula for success. Too many stars who are seeking individual accolades will relegate a team to failure. A team with players that defer individual glory for the success of the team will eventually take home the "brass ring."

Despite differences of location and demographic composition, schools and school districts are somewhat the same operationally. While they may share operational issues such as schedules, busing, and other such mandates, they are, at the same time, very different instructionally with their own unique internal dynamics.

When building a team, the leader must be cognizant of how the individual members fit together and the situation in which they will be working. While the "one size fits all" approach may work in generic situations, schools or districts seeking to improve performance recognize that specific attributes and skills of team members must complement one another.

Jay Wright, Villanova Head Basketball Coach and winner of two national titles, indicates that it is essential to identify personnel that will fit your system.[7] Wright recognizes that there are great players that just do not have the social emotional "make-up" and maturity to do the things that they are asked to do. Ultimately, his players have talent to compete almost anywhere but it is the element of team, selflessness, and the mental mindset to sacrifice personal gain for the betterment of the team that makes the difference.

We also sought those that are willing to give off themselves for the betterment of the team. We actively sought individuals who want to be part of something bigger than themselves. It was also recognized that an organization will only reach a synergistic level of performance when it is built around members who work collaboratively to elevate the skills of those around them so that the team's performance outcomes can be achieved. The prize is not one of individual accolades or awards but rather improving performance for ALL children.

SUMMARY

- Recruitment and hiring are high stakes activities that can improve performance if structured and designed properly.
- Build flexibility into the selection process.
- Maintaining the interpersonal aspects of the selection process allows the team to discover qualities that contribute to performance.
- Adept leaders recognize that the selection process of personnel is strategic.
- The process can result in a candidate that infuses positive energy into the organization and builds internal capacity.

RECOMMENDATIONS

- Focus on criteria that build a team-oriented culture.
- Fine-tune the existing interview strategies, rubrics, and technology in the search and interview process to reflect the criteria that will produce personnel that will flourish in a performance-based culture.
- Incorporate the key characteristics of Attitude, Character, Skills, and Demonstrated Success into the process.
- Understand how each selection and personnel placement must be an optimal fit to the organization's existing system to produce maximum outcomes.
- Recognize that organizational chemistry is the formula for success.

ACTIVITIES

- Examine "Teacher Perceiver" instrument or other hiring rubrics.
- Complete Appendix B#6: Critique of Hiring Process.
- Determine if there is a correlation between high performing staff members and the college/university from which they graduated.

Chapter 5

The Transition to Higher Performance

When a leader is considering the challenge of moving a school or district to one which is focused on achievement and higher performance, the leader must be cognizant that the task is a daunting one. It is clearly a path lined with choices, decisions, obstacles, and risks. Choosing wisely and being strategic can make the difference between success and failure. Being arbitrary and non-inclusive can result in a massive morale problem which may be insurmountable and impact any future efforts or adjustments.

Numerous scholars and researchers have studied the journey by documenting the factors involved in the organizational change process along with the complexity of it. One such researcher, Michael Fullan, Dean of the Ontario Institute for Studies, examined the culture of change[1] and the forces of change[2] which challenged the traditional theory on organizational reform. Conclusions offered by Fullan as well as other researchers offer a litany of variables that can lead to a successful outcome but the common denominator in each scenario always includes effective leadership. In the case of a leader seeking to transition a school or district, the leader must possess and demonstrate specific skills.

LEADERSHIP PROCESS SKILLS

Confident

A leader must be confident that the pathway or plan that is selected will lead to the desired outcome. The leader's confidence must be based on definable outcomes that are really supported by concrete data and research. It must be based on evidence and facts versus conjecture and opinion. An event illustrating how confidence can make a difference occurred when we examined performance at the high school.

Due to a variety of reasons, the high school was lagging behind the district in overall student performance. It suffered from a "crisis of leadership" resulting from interim appointments who acted as "placeholders." The interim leaders were appointed and maintained the "status quo" until we found a candidate capable of leading the school in another direction. Each interim appointment was a capable leader in the traditional sense but they were not tasked or expected to change the current climate. They were only going to hold the position for a short duration of time. After several failed searches, we identified a candidate that had the demeanor to lead the initiative to improve the high school's performance.

Without leadership and direction, the high school staff had grown accustomed to being fiercely independent. When seeking input from the staff regarding qualities which they desired in a new principal, they almost unanimously listed leadership, but what they really wanted was leadership on their terms. The new candidate would have to be savvy enough to maneuver this group in the direction of improving performance without alienating them.

After much research we decided to attend an open house at Adlai Stevenson High School in Lincolnshire, Illinois, with the new appointee. Under the leadership of Dr. Richard DeFour, Stevenson High School had acquired a reputation of excellence so we thought that it was a good starting point. The school was a high performing organization with "cutting edge" programs that delivered excellent outcomes. The plan was to actually observe what was indeed possible.

Two days later, when we debriefed at a nearby hotel conference room, the newly appointed principal indicated, with tears in her eyes, that she did not think that it was possible to meet our expectations. It was explained that she would not be alone and that we would accomplish this task together.

She not only met our expectations but exceeded them on a number of levels. With the confidence of actually observing real outcomes and with the confidence that she had the support of the superintendent, the central office, and the board, she proceeded to design an outstanding plan that was inclusive and collaborative and one that produced real results.

Confidence is not about false bravado but rather is substantive. It is about having the knowledge to know what is possible, designing a plan, communicating the plan, and implementing it.

Facilitation

To transition to a high performing school environment, the leader must be adept at facilitating a conversation about the change process which focuses on improvement. There is a variety of significant stakeholders which must be nurtured for the plan to succeed. It is important to utilize an approach which provides them with the knowledge, data, and information that jettisons the past in favor of a future with better outcomes. Leaders must, therefore, understand how to build a consensus among these stakeholders toward a common purpose and an objective which was developed with stakeholder input.

Discussions with faculty and staff regarding improvement can often be emotionally laden. Faculty and staff who have been vested in the current status quo are reluctant to break with the past practice. In many cases, teachers and staff may be very good at delivering the existing curriculum and instruction, even though it may not be producing improved results. Any change for this group may be perceived as a threat to their professionalism.

Even though their children would appear to be clear beneficiaries to a higher performing environment, parents, depending on their motivation, may express concerns about a focus on improved achievement. The parents of high achieving children may want to maintain the status quo at the expense of lower achieving students. A skilled facilitator must maneuver both groups toward a belief that all children will benefit from such an agenda and that no one's potential will be compromised in the process.

Other stakeholders such as board members may become anxious when pressured by constituents who claim the proposed changes may unnecessarily "rock the boat." Still other board members may need assurances because of the political risk that such a change may represent.

Remember, at the core of each board member is the heart of a politician. While responsible to a constituency that elected them, they may be reluctant to embrace an agenda that shifts the district's focus and possibly even their role.

Managing the desires and psyche of all stakeholders is a challenge. It again requires an adept leader who is a facilitator and is strategic. The leader understands the importance of forming a group with the proper chemistry that will "get the job done" and maintain the fundamental tenets of the mission. They inherently know when to push and when to get out of the way.

Adept facilitators are synergistic. They know when to bring a group together, resolve issues within the group, and when to assist. Most importantly, leaders who are good facilitators allow a group to work independently but at the same time know how to monitor their activity without being authoritative or intrusive.

Adept leaders, through structured discussions and meetings, can demonstrate that they are part of the team but no more important than any other member of it. A skilled facilitator knows how to reinforce the principles of performance without being overbearing.

Every ten years the high school participated in an accreditation process. As a new principle, we opted for a new protocol, "Accreditation for Growth," because it was more consistent with our emerging continuous improvement philosophy. The new protocol focused more on achievement goals than the traditional protocol which examined the quality of the facility and its staff.

Like any such process, the key was in the selection of a chairperson. Generally, an administrator who could bring stakeholders together was a priority because much of the process involved staff members responding to written questions. The responses were compiled in a report for the visiting accreditation team. The review team would also interview the stakeholders in an attempt to further validate the responses.

Since everyone's administrative plate was full and no one was enthusiastic about taking on such a task, the responsibility of selecting a chair from the administrative team was a difficult decision. It may have been easier to go outside of the team and widen the selection process, but we were at the early stages of building a continuous improvement process. We were still in a transition phase, but nonetheless we realized that this process could catapult us down the road to laying the foundation to better performance.

The selected chairperson was a gregarious administrator, but unfortunately lacked the internal organizational skills to build stakeholder committees that were instructionally focused. The chair was fairly new to administration and never made the accreditation process a priority. With only a few weeks before the actual team visit, the chair informed us that the process was languishing. The only way to meet the timeline was for the principal to assume total responsibility for its completion. We ultimately did well, but it was a hard lesson to learn.

Always select a facilitator with the required skills to accomplish a complex activity. Do not select the most convenient option available. We were lucky and were able to intervene in a timely manner.

Determination

Given the "high pressure" environment that a transition to higher performance can create, it is easy to be dissuaded from the end goal of improved student achievement. These internal and external pressures are probably one of the main reasons that leaders often avoid the challenge of improving performance. When in the throes of transitioning a school or district to higher performance, the subtle and overt maneuvering of stakeholders, particularly in the early stages of the process, might have any leader questioning the logic of entertaining an idea for a change of this magnitude.

In this type of environment, leaders must have the skill to resolve issues without modifying the overall objective. As an adept leader, they should have the latitude to modify the how but not the why or the designated outcome. Stakeholders may try to maneuver a leader away from the objective, but the leader must be able to "outflank" those maneuvers to keep the process moving forward toward its goals.

The state mandated a graduation project. It was not popular among the faculty who felt overwhelmed by the already increased expectations of teaching and learning. There was a myriad of questions: Who would grade it? Who would monitor it? How would it apply to diverse student learning styles?

As the principal and chair of the committee which was comprised of the high school's content department chairs, it was evident that there were individuals on the committee whose agenda was to prevent the project from seeing the "light of day" or minimally deferring it long enough so that it would "die a slow death." It was also clear from the central office that they wanted it done.

We eventually implemented the graduation project and it was a huge success. It happened because we maintained our focus and allowed the chairs to design the project to meet the curriculum nuances of each department. In the end, the final project was far more creative and imaginative than any administratively designed project would have been.

Leaders have to be unwavering toward the goal but flexible in the approach of how the team gets there. Determination to reach the goal and an unwavering commitment to get there are essential ingredients in an adept leader that understands the performance improvement process.

POSITIONING FOR PERFORMANCE

Schools and districts often require significant foundation building before actually beginning a process of improvement. Very few administrators, teachers, and staff line up outside the superintendent's office waiting to discuss how they can assist in the process. More often than not, there are the questions of Why? How? And Is this really possible?

To combat this skepticism about any performance-related initiative, research and responsibility for its outcomes are the prescribed antidotes. These antidotes build an urgency to change. Facts and data open the internal pathways of the organization for such change to occur.

Research

There is no better research than the data which is readily available in every school or district. With the advent of data warehousing, there are troves of information to analyze. The key to this analysis is the ability to interpret the data and determine which factors have the greatest impact on achievement.

Often, there is a tendency to examine social and demographic factors which are beyond the control of the school or district. If the analysis of those factors is limited to data generated as a result of student work during the school day rather than those beyond the confines of the school building, the eventual development of goals and actions plans will be more realistic. The analysis of data associated with teaching and learning eliminates excuses, creates accountability, and develops inclusive responsibility.

Faculty and staff are also more likely to be compelled to move in another direction when the research highlights a pathway that will improve instruction in their classroom. Teachers want students to achieve. Concrete evidence of students, who are similar to those students in their classroom, is more likely to convince them to endorse the new approach.

Even for those teachers that cling to past practice for convenience or belief, concrete examples of dramatic growth and achievement are compelling examples to emulate. When a process in which data, research, and examples of real growth are disseminated, this information can become the catalyst to change and outmaneuver any resistance to it.

There was a great deal of skepticism among some long standing and respected faculty members at the middle school when there was a discussion to change the mathematics curriculum. The new program involved more engagement and abstraction. The resistance movement was strong but dissipated when those teachers saw the dramatic improvement of elementary students who participated in a similar program. The elementary students were learning algebraic concepts, working in teams, solving complex word problems, and explaining solutions.

There was no denying that the new methodology and curriculum were successful at the elementary level. Long-held convictions gave way to demonstrated examples of achievement. Another undeniable fact was that these students were moving to the middle school and the expectations were now higher. Change was no longer an option for those in the path of improved student achievement.

Shared Responsibility

Educators want students to achieve and to have those students prepared for success in the world. With this inherent belief, those leading the initiative to improve performance should appeal to one's moral responsibility to move from a "status quo" position of underperformance or mediocrity to an approach that attempts to improve student outcomes. To continue to utilize the same methodology and curriculum to produce a different result, "year in and year out," is inconceivable.

Low expectations are also a benign practice that kills student achievement. A combination of an irrelevant curriculum, poor methodology, and low expectations over a number of years can doom students to failure. In essence, all stakeholders have a moral responsibility to change the cycle of failure. It is a compelling argument that all stakeholders can endorse.

With increased expectations there is increased responsibility, but that responsibility is shared both individually and collectively. The superintendent, the central office, building administrators, and support staff share the responsibility for a child's success or failure. While teachers are key members in a delivery process, teachers are not to assume total responsibility for success of the process. The role of principals, supervisors, and others is to provide the necessary support so that those directly delivering instruction are successful. Logically, if support is provided to those who are at the "tip of the spear" in delivering the process, then the students will succeed.

To further share responsibility, we examined how buildings were scheduled and how students were grouped. Previously, some buildings grouped all of the advanced students together and a majority of the failing or "at risk" children together. It was obvious that such a design contributed to a lack of collaboration and "buy-in" to building goals.

By eliminating this practice, particularly at the elementary level, all children were now exposed to higher expectations at a younger age. All staff members were also now vested in the learning outcomes for underachieving students at the building level. Staff members were now driven to collaborate to raise student performance levels for all children.

Sometimes, it is also strategic to "find the seam" that all stakeholders can support. It was one such seam that provided our pathway to improvement. If we were to succeed, it would be as a group. If we failed, we failed as a group. The following briefly illustrates that scenario:

The board created a merit pay plan to improve performance in a unilateral manner. As a new superintendent who inherited the plan, it was easy to note the flaws in the system and to plan for an option which would be more palatable and possibly more collaborative. What essentially was missing from the merit plan was a system of collective accountability.

All groups could embrace the concept of team, grade level or building accountability. While there was significant derision for the existing merit pay plan, once a collective plan was implemented, the objections dissipated. Groups began to work together and proceeded to "unlock the silos" and experience the synergy of collaboration.

Creating a team approach and providing the tools for success will further position those in both leadership and delivery roles to endorse a plan for improved performance. By supporting the relocation of resources for professional development and by providing other tangible supports, key stakeholders will also demonstrate that they are invested in the process.

FRAMEWORK FOR PERFORMANCE

While stakeholders will question why and who is ultimately responsible for an endeavor such as improving performance, not far behind those loaded inquiries are questions of how are we going to accomplish such a task. Most of those stakeholders will want information on the design or the framework to improve performance.

As indicated in "Performance Is Key,"[3] there are many quality designs that will assist in improving effectiveness, such as the Baldrige Education Performance program,[4] Lezotte's "Correlates for Effective Schools,"[5] or John Doerr's "Objective and Key Results" (OKR),[6] but for stakeholders to support a process which involves self-examination and the potential for major reform, the process must be individually tailored.

Since most plans "do not survive the point of initial review,"[7] customization makes the plan more acceptable to those most threatened by such a reform. It has been our experience that an internally developed administrative framework which allows customization to the process demonstrates flexibility and collaboration. A plan that combines local expertise with grounded research increases its appeal to internal stakeholders.

By allowing and planning for input, the administration sends a signal of willingness to work together and respect the contributions of the professionals in the organization. At the same time, process leaders cannot allow the design and framework to deviate from the performance principles. For the most part, stakeholders will endorse a design that incorporates the following components:

- Customized
- Data driven
- Goal oriented
- Outcomes based
- Internal accountability
- Shared responsibility

Even with the most altruistic of motivations which focus on improving performance for all children, some members of an organization may attempt to undermine the intent of the design. While remaining positive, adept leaders must recognize that there is often an underground network of communication within the school or district to which the process leader has no access. This network is informal and communication is generally verbal. It is limited to those with similar positions and those of "like minds."

We'd call them the "rumblings." When several members of an internal network started to position themselves to oppose a direction, action, or potential action, these "rumblings" weren't necessarily a good thing. It represented some sort of "push back" regarding an initiative which if it gained momentum could become problematic. What we did recognize was that we needed to ascertain what the "rumblings" were about and get ahead of any formal mobilization.

One such "rumbling" began early in the morning as the result of a board directive requiring that all faculty members monitor at least two "after school" events a year. Actually, it was the result of a clumsy and poorly written component of a new teacher contract, but it was a radical departure from past practice. The union agreed to the provision because they never thought that it would take place, but the board reminded the administrative team of its responsibility to implement this provision. The unofficial word from the network was that we, the administration, were going to arbitrarily assign faculty members to cover activities.

Even though administrators probably had the latitude to just assign staff to an activity, we heard the "rumbling" in advance of any petition or filing of a grievance. We worked out a selection system based on seniority that met the spirit of the agreement. By doing so we eliminated a distraction to our efforts associated with improving the culture, thus averting a crisis of morale and trust.

It is important to know what those outside the planning circle are thinking. By "placing your ear to the ground" and listening to those willing to share, an adept leader can circumvent potential issues which are being discussed in this network. By proactively distributing information or making announcements which further clarify the process and delineating the roles within it, identifying areas for improvement and transparently discussing other expressed issues of concern, a leader can quickly turn a potential negative into a positive.

Getting ahead of potential issues before they become a major obstacle is both strategic and synergistic. By eliminating the "background noise," the leader keeps the organization focused on its mission of high performance and learning for ALL students.

SUMMARY

- The transition to higher performance requires leaders who are adept and savvy.
- Adept Leaders have the confidence to produce outcomes that represent higher achievement for ALL children.

- Performance process leaders must have strong facilitation skills to build a consensus among a variety of stakeholders.
- Determination is an essential quality in a leader seeking to change the "status quo."
- Positioning a school or district for performance requires research and developing a shared sense of responsibility.
- Designing a framework for performance optimally seeks input from stakeholders.
- Process leaders cannot allow the design and framework to deviate from the defined performance principles.
- Stakeholders will endorse a design that incorporates specific components (such as Customization, Data Driven, Goal Orientation, Outcomes Based, Internal Accountability, and Shared Responsibility) if they are designed collaboratively.
- Proactive leaders are strategic and synergistic.

RECOMMENDATIONS

- Select a leader who has the ability to instill confidence in the process, build consensus, and is both determined and committed to improving achievement.
- Build a sense of urgency for change through research, data, and concrete models of success.
- Alleviate stakeholder concerns by building a system of shared responsibility.
- Develop a framework that permits internal input and feedback in the design.
- Remain positive and proactive when dealing with resistance to the process.

ACTIVITIES

- Survey colleagues to determine the qualities of an Effective Leader.
- Complete *Appendix B* #7: Mandate to Improve.

Chapter 6

Guiding the Process

Unlike other sporting venues, baseball fields are unique due to their design and layout. The distance and configuration of the walls and fences are not uniform. Prior to each baseball game, the umpires and coaches from each respective team gather at home plate to discuss the "ground rules" for playing in the stadium. The conversation is an effort to understand what constitutes a home run or foul ball in each stadium. The goal is to create an atmosphere where rules are applied in a consistent manner.

For a leader to orchestrate a plan to improve performance, all participates should be cognizant of the "ground rules" that can make the process a productive one. Understanding the rules keeps the discussions for improvement focused and the associated problem-solving process targeted.

FACTS VS. OPINIONS

The process of improving performance in a school or district is a complex one, which requires the inclusion of all stakeholders. Seeking collaborative input from multiple sources and verifying the accuracy of that information is critical in targeting the areas which necessitate improvement. On the surface, building a consensus around identified deficiencies and developing a plan for remediating them appear simple and routine.

Contrary to this perception is the reality that internal politics and "power plays" can "ground" even the worthiest of initiatives to a halt. Even though it can become cumbersome, all stakeholders from all organizational levels must have input into the process and have some form of representation at the table.

School board meetings were always uncharted territory when it came to audience participation and commentary. Having board members understand the improvement process and its "ground rules" helped in keeping the conversation focused. Fortunately, my board president always had a clarifying rule: "You have a right to your opinion but not the facts."

While all opinions are clearly respected, the process must remain focused by examining the merits of such opinions with facts, data, and research. Speculation is not an option. Facts, data, and research are the controlling factors in any discussion.

LISTEN

Everybody wants everything done yesterday! Yet, the most critical and "time consuming" process is listening. Skipping this step will doom the performance initiative to failure.

Slowing down, listening, and reflecting have saved us from making mistakes. Most administrators perceive themselves are "doers." Most leaders want to get it done quickly and move on to the next issue, crisis, or planning session. It often feels like there's no time to waste when the paperwork, telephone calls, or emails are pressuring you to do something. High-pressure situations often require investigation, research, and verification.

The performance process is no different. There is often much to sort out after a discussion, particularly with a group of stakeholders. Slow down and reflect before reacting.

LARGE TO SMALL

To ensure that all voices and perspectives are heard, initially, a larger group is certainly better than a smaller group. Discussing the process with a large group of key communicators reinforces a sense of inclusion and respect. Once feedback from the larger groups is obtained, then smaller organizational groups can help to sort out the information.

From our perspective, teacher groups from internal organizational levels (K–3, 4–5, 6–8, 9–12) were most beneficial because they could pinpoint issues that affect them directly and allow leaders to react to those specific issues. By grouping board, central office administrators, principals, teachers (elementary, middle, secondary), and support staff in separate groups, a non-threatening environment or "safe zone" is created for real discussion. Given the number of staff in large schools or districts, it may be more productive to limit participation to key instructional leaders.

SURVEY

Prior to coordinating meetings to ascertain feedback, it is advisable for each organizational group (board, central office, principals, teachers by building, etc.) and other supervisory groups to complete the *"School Systems Cross Check"* (see *Appendix A* #1). The results of the *"Cross Check"* will be tabulated, verified, and clarified for accuracy at follow-up meetings with those groups. The data from the survey may yield many systemic disconnections which when further analyzed will reveal more specific obstacles to teaching, learning, and student performance.

The next time you take a flight, take a moment to observe the preflight process that is taking place on the plane prior to departing the gate. While passengers are busily being seated, the pilots are checking systems to ensure that everything is functioning properly.

On a plane there are a variety of systems that must function properly for the plane to reach peak performance. Many of these complex systems are dependent on each other with a level of redundancy built into them to prevent any major malfunction. The gauges in the cockpit act as primary indicators of performance but as most pilots would argue, there are subtle features in handling the plane that can forewarn those in control that performance is being impeded in some way.

Much like in aviation, education has many moving and interrelated components. While attending exclusively to one component may contribute to better performance, the interrelationships of these components establish the connections which make higher performance possible. When the organization is "running on all eight cylinders," a synergy of effort unleashes internal creativity and capacity. Only when organizational decision making, resource allocation, methodological application, and instruction are all laser-focused on maximizing student potential will growth be exponential.

A survey such as the *"School Systems Cross Check"* provides the leadership with the data to identify the disconnections and obstacles to improving student achievement by examining four major components and over 100 additional factors that contribute to performance. The four components and the associated factors are as follows: Alignment, Atmosphere, Accountability and Adept Leadership.

The relationship of these components and factors is further examined in the context of a stakeholder's perception of the strength of each elemental component and achievement factor within the organization. Data from the instrument further provides the leadership team with information necessary to link all school systems to each other in a manner that generates collaborative growth and higher performance while utilizing existing resources.

Alignment	
Structure	Practices
Policies	Regulations/Documents
Framework Design	Customized/Personalized
	Analytical/Targeted
	Improvement Orientation
	Systemic
Strategic Planning	Mission, Values, Beliefs
	Cross-Division Goals
	Embeddedness
	Data Driven, Measurable
	Action Planning
	Targets/Indicators/Outcomes
	Monitoring/Evaluation
Instructional Focus	Methodology
	Skill Development
	Resource Allocation
Systems Effectiveness	Operational Interconnectedness
Communication	Transparency, Stakeholder

Attitude/Atmosphere	
Structure	Practices
Policies	Regulations/Documents
Values/Beliefs	Students/Faculty/Staff
	Stakeholders
Attitude	Positivity
	Resilience
	Collaboration/Team Work
	"Buy-In"
	Empowerment
	Synergy
Personnel	Support Processes
	Inclusiveness
	Problem Solving
	Recognition
Professional Development	Tiered
	Career Development
	Teacher Leaders
	Skill Development
	Coaching/Mentoring
Hiring	Recruitment
	Interview Process
	Orientation

Accountability	
Structure	*Practices*
Policies	Regulations/Documents
System of Assessment	Method of Measurement
	Multiple Sources of Data
	Measurable
	Defined Expectations
	Data Review Process
	Collaborative
	Data Review Process
	Reporting Transparency
	Data Warehousing
Shared Accountability	Multi-Level, Individual
	Collective
	Differentiated Goals
	Flexibility
	Check/Balances
	Monitoring Procedures
	Review Process
Evaluation	Observation/Supervision Process
	Organizationally Connected
	Summative (Summary)
	Formative (Developmental)
	Intervention
	Progressive

Adept Leadership	
Structure	*Practices*
Policies	Regulations/Documents
Leadership	Substantive vs. Superficial
	Visionary
	Motivational
	Consensus Building/Collaborative
	Decision Maker
	Risk Taker
	Achievement Priority/Focus
	Problem Solver
	Team Builder
Management Style	Success/Task/Outcomes Oriented
	Knowledgeable/Skilled
	Values Contributions/Teamwork
	Empowers
	Mentors/Models/Nurtures
	Engages Stakeholders

(Continued)

(Continued)

Structure	Adept Leadership
	Practices
Instructional Focus	Accepts Responsibility
	Equitable/Fair
	Communicates
	Recognizes Contributions
	Empathetic
	Goal/Success Oriented
	Understands Methodology
	Practical
	Flexible
	Inclusive
	Focus on Improvement
Outreach	Macro/Micro
	Business/Agencies

Much like the pilots who are "crosschecking" system performance during preflight to assure maximum performance, we encourage leadership teams to "Cross Check" a school system's vital components, so that maximum performance is reached. In the end, a district's flight path is dependent on the ability of its pilots to manage its systems.

APPRECIATE

When beginning the process of improving performance, it is also critical to become familiar with the traditions within an organization and to acknowledge the efforts of the professionals within it. To totally ignore past efforts and contributions to improve performance may be perceived as disrespectful and possibly arrogant by the "hard working" staff members that have tried to make the school or district better. Nothing will mobilize resistance to change or a reform initiative faster than the appearance of having all the answers.

A better approach attempts to ascertain the positive aspects and results from past efforts by dialoguing with all stakeholders. This approach, sometimes referred to as *Appreciative Inquiry*,[1] is a starting point in any discussion (see *Appendix A* #6). It acknowledges the efforts of all those that preceded the current leadership team and attempts to "build bridges" and trust.

We began every board retreat with an appreciative inquiry activity. We always focused on the positive before examining the issues. It was then followed by a Gallery Walk.

With the previously distributed colored "sticky notes" in-hand, we encouraged both board members and administrators to collaboratively rank the positives and negatives in the district by placing the notes on the wall under specific headings. Each colored note was correlated to a high or low ranking. While tabulations were easy to do, the patterns and trends immediately jumped off the conference room walls. It was not only interesting to ascertain the board's perspectives but it empowered them. The activity reinforced our concept of stakeholders seeking solutions together.

When seeking group stakeholder input, always do so in a controlled setting where dialogue is possible. Rarely is everything wrong within a school or organization. Stakeholders will offer both positive and negative perspectives. Initially, it is worth acknowledging the positive before untangling the negative. Those leaders who perceive that the "glass is empty" and not worth saving may find that there is no one remaining within the organization willing to assist in the journey toward improvement.

"CHECKS AND BALANCES"

With "shared responsibility" there must be shared power for all participants to have a stake in the process. Inclusionary models often tout the value of shared responsibility but few provide those with the responsibility for delivering the outcomes with any power in the decision-making process.

For "shared power" to become a reality, a system of *"checks and balances"* should be considered. When these "checks and balances" are embedded in the performance design, the decision-making process becomes a shared one. The formation of *District Improvement* and *School Improvement Teams* can assist in creating an atmosphere of shared decision making and empowerment. These teams should be formed with a cross-section of personnel with diverse skills and responsibility, not to exceed 8–12 individuals.[2]

District teams are responsible for analysis and diagnosis of both systemic and organizational level factors impacting overall performance but should not have absolute control over prioritization and implementation at the building level. Both district and building level teams are required to interface and collaborate on the final selection of the factors that have the greatest impact on instruction.

Even within this system of "checks and balances," there is one caveat. The superintendent of schools has the final authority in resolving disputes associated with findings, expectations, and outcomes. It is also clearly beneficial and collaborative to resolve such disputes by examining the guiding performance principles, the data, and the relevant research.

Process leaders are mindful of the organization's dynamics and are strategic in the resolution of issues. Spending time orienting the team regarding its mission and reviewing performance principles with both district and building teams provides them with guidance and focus. In doing so, needless sidetracking and delays can be avoided.

ANALYSIS

If a survey process (i.e., *"Cross Check"*) is utilized along with initial and subsequent stakeholder discussions to verify information, a significant number of factors that impact performance will be generated. When school/district policies and procedures are examined in conjunction with achievement data, the accumulation of data can be significant and can be overwhelming. Just determining how to organize the information can stall the investigative process.

Data will require categorization and may even require formal statistical treatment to determine patterns and trends. At the same time, the process leader should not succumb to "analysis paralysis." The process leader must consider in the design not only how the data will be analyzed but who will conduct the analysis prior to commencing its acquisition.

Prior to the analysis of data consider the role of the *District Improvement Team* in guiding the analytical phase. The district team may have greater expertise to better analyze the data at both the district and building level. Composition of this team should include those with the analytical capability to do so. Team members for consideration include the superintendent, assistant superintendent, curriculum supervisors, technology coordinators, and others familiar with statistical analysis.

Only after extensive analysis, research, and verification should the district team present its results to the board, building level teams, and other stakeholders. At this point anyone can contest the findings but must do so with factually based research rather than emotionally laden perceptions.

DIAGNOSIS

While analysis may highlight the various obstacles and impediments impacting achievement of a school or district, particular care must be given to the diagnosis. Where analysis may highlight the symptoms to underperformance, the diagnosis attempts to define a cause-and-effect relationship to them. In doing so, district team analysis may highlight systemic, organizational level and building specific concerns.

Toward the conclusion of its analysis, the district team may want to confer and collaborate with each *School Improvement Building Team* to further validate its findings. The district team very easily might have misinterpreted a data cell or weighed a factor too heavily. The old adage, "the more eyes looking at it the better," builds collaboration toward an accurate diagnosis. At the same time, strategic leaders must be cognizant regarding the quality of the analysis and the team's conclusions.

Conclusions and recommendations must always be supported by research and data. Rather than succumb to the loudest and most outspoken voices, those who utilize reason, logic, facts, and data should prevail. When the teams arrive at a consensus regarding the diagnosis, the subsequent recommendations are only approved after review by the superintendent. It is only then that the process of prioritization should begin.

The parameters to prioritization limit the consideration of extraneous factors. Logically, why prioritize issues and potential solutions beyond one's control that will never make the "cut."

PRIORITIZATION

After spending a substantial amount of time examining and analyzing the issues, then differentiating those issues in terms of causation, most members of an improvement team either want to complete them all at one time or lobby on behalf of those issues in which they have a strong conviction. Trying to remediate everything at one time will ultimately result in a drain of resources and total confusion. Having a conviction about an issue or solution is admirable, but that conviction may not be accurate and the solution may be beyond the scope of the school or district.

Poverty or socioeconomic factors contribute directly to achievement, but a school or district will not be able to resolve them. Certainly, there are opportunities in which a school or district can lessen the impact of such influences, but the school or district must limit its priorities to those instructional issues that it can control during the school day. A process leader who is a facilitator must get "everyone on the same page" and moving in the same direction.

By utilizing a number of techniques including the "Pareto Principle,"[3] the process leader might be able to provide a "laser focus" to the prioritization process. Pareto gets team members to invoke the "80–20" rule. The process states that, for many events, roughly 80% of the effects come from 20% of the causes. For instance, one may believe more state or federal money is the answer, but it may only be a contributing factor. There may be more tangible factors in which a school or district has greater control which may make a more significant difference.

Pareto and other decision-making tools assist leaders in effectively directing resources to areas that will have the greatest impact. Professional development and curriculum initiatives are such areas. When priorities are clearly defined in each area and aligned with the performance initiative, instructional consistency is more likely.

PRESCRIPTION

When the factors impacting performance are identified and prioritized, the improvement teams need to examine the complexity of those factors and the duration that the remediation of those factors might require. Variables such as professional capacity, resource availability, and reallocation, as well as training, are just a few areas for consideration. Other issues involving curriculum development and instructional methodology may require board approval along with changes to policies and procedures that may be hindering performance.

The district was spending a substantial amount of its budget on personal professional growth. The board was increasingly frustrated that teachers were accelerating through the salary scale by acquiring a Masters or Doctorate degree. Yet, there appeared to be no apparent correlation between advanced degrees and increased student achievement.

Upon further examination it was determined that the faculty had the latitude to enroll in an array of unrelated courses to obtain a Masters Equivalency or in a Doctoral program that required little more than 6 months of online engagement. Closing this loophole allowed us to align our professional development program to the performance initiative and to build our internal capacity related to our mission.

From our perspective, systemic issues were always a priority due to the overarching effect that they might have on a school or district. Disconnections associated with the alignment of an organization, its culture, the system of accountability, and of course, its leadership, could adversely impact achievement in a number of ways.

"The whole is greater to the sum of its parts," and the manner in which key factors or parts interact with each other can either improve or hinder performance. Making those issues a priority is important. Of course, depending on the complexity of these items, timelines for completion may vary. For example, some items have threads that are implemented vertically into every level but are phased-in through a multi-year process. Getting all of the parts to mesh in an effective manner takes time.

Understanding what works and what does not is essential to the improvement process. Identifying the obstacles to improvement and developing a cohesive plan which is integrated will result in increased performance for the organization and the students that it serves. Adept leaders are those skilled in utilizing an improvement process that is collaborative, analytical, and holds all stakeholders accountable for its results.

SUMMARY

- Adherence to the components of the Performance Process will ensure an inclusive, collaborative, and analytical approach to improvement.
- Facts, data, and research are the controlling factors in a discussion to improve performance.
- Listening provides an internal perspective of organizational dynamics, issues, and previous attempts to remediate issues of underperformance.
- Large to small organizational discussion group increases feedback and verification.
- Survey first and then verify results through discussion groups.
- Recognize past attempts at improvement before examining organizational deficiencies.
- A system of "checks and balances" empowers those delivering and implementing the initiative.
- Analysis pinpoints factors or "disconnections" that may impede performance.
- Diagnosis defines a "cause and effect" relationship to poor performance.
- Prioritization maximizes resource utilization and human capital in the effort to improve a school or district.

RECOMMENDATIONS

- Create a design that involves District and School Improvement Teams.
- Develop a system of "checks and balances."
- Listen before reacting.
- Be strategic in organizing discussion groups and the District and School Improvement teams and in the selection of analytical personnel.
- Prioritization techniques will result in a more efficient and effective process.
- Synergistic concepts of inclusion and collaboration always outweigh exclusion and isolation.

ACTIVITIES

- Review *Appendix A* #1: School Systems "Cross Check."
- Review *Appendix A* #6 and #7: Board of Directors/Administrative Retreat Framework.
- Complete *Appendix B* #8: "80–20" Rule.

Part III

FANNING THE FLAMES

"Success is a Journey, Not a Destination"

—Ben Sweetland

In this section of *Igniting Performance*, the focus shifts from developing the fundamental groundwork and analytical process to actual implementation. Procedures, designs, and structures are discussed along with aligning professional development to goals and action plans. While successful implementation is important, sustaining the initiative is equally a major consideration. Case Studies will provide actual insight into the Performance Improvement Process. It is one thing to light a fire, but it is another to keep the flame alive.

Chapter 7

Implementation Strategies for Success

DISTRICT AND SCHOOL IMPROVEMENT TEAMS

As previously indicated, *District and School Improvement Teams* are the structural force in the identification and analysis of the factors contributing to the underperformance of a school or school district. These teams create the "road map that determines the changes within a school or district for improvement regarding the level of student achievement."[1]

During the analytical and diagnostic process, the teams conferred with each other regarding the results. The teams discuss the relevance of each identified issue and further verify those issues through dialogue, data, and research as it applies to the district and the building level.

With the prioritization of issues and developing a consensus around the importance of each factor's impact on performance, the district team develops general goals for improvement and subsets of those goals for the district. These goals are transferable to all levels of the organization, but the process allows each organizational level to develop *Action Plans* to meet them.

In other words, the district team recommends the overall instructional goals for the district but the buildings have flexibility on how to meet them. Such a process ensures consistency in the implementation process across the district but allows customization in the writing of *Action Plans* at the building level in meeting the designated building goals.

DISTRICT GOAL APPROVAL PROCESS

The caveat of this structure is that the superintendent, upon reviewing the goals, determines the increment or percentage of growth for each building in the organization. Following the review of the district's goals, there is a presentation to the school board, initially at the committee level and later for formal approval at a board meeting. These district goals also become the instructional goals of the superintendent and become part of their evaluation process.

By incorporating the school board into the approval process, stakeholders are again encouraged to participate. In many school districts, board members are far removed from the goal development process for fear of micromanagement. Additionally, it is rare for a superintendent to link real concrete instructional results and outcomes to their evaluation process.

Transparency in the approval process increases opportunities for stakeholder participation. The direct transference of these goals to the superintendent's evaluation sends a message of shared responsibility. The burden for the delivery of the targeted outcomes does not just fall on the shoulders of the teachers but rather on everyone in the organization.

GOALS

The utilization of goals in the improvement process is a fairly standard practice but surprisingly few adhere to specific criteria in the development of them. Each goal must be attainable and measurable. Each goal and subsequent *Action Plan* require the assignment of an individual or group to monitor them at the designated operational level for accountability as well as assuming responsibility for their completion.

Too often, there is a tendency to target too many goals in an instructional area. Goals should target no more than three broad areas otherwise the organization's effectiveness in completing those goals is diminished. A sample for a district goal and its corresponding building goal is provided as follows:

EXAMPLE

District Improvement Goals

1. Seventy percent of the students in the "Ideal School District" will be proficient as demonstrated on standardized "X" assessment.

Subset Goals

a. The district will improve reading and mathematics proficiency at all school district organizational levels (K–3, 4–5, 6–8, 9–12) by a minimum of "X" percent* as demonstrated on standardized "X" assessment compared to the previous year's results.

   (*percentages of designated growth will vary by building)

Building Goals

"Ideal" Elementary School

1. The "Ideal" Elementary School will improve reading proficiency by "X" percent* as demonstrated by "X" assessment as compared to the previous year's assessment.

   (*the superintendent will negotiate the exact percentage of growth depending on the challenges and instructional variables within each school)

Subset Goal

a. The school will improve reading comprehension as evidenced by demonstrated increased proficiency on standardized "X" assessment.
b. The school will improve inferential reading skills as evidenced by demonstrated growth on standardized "X" assessment.
c. The school will improve non-fiction reading skills as evidenced by demonstrated growth on standardized "X" assessment specific to this skill.

The planning for mathematics goals or other identified instructional goals followed a similar pattern. The district goals were broader in scope but definitive in the overall expectations for growth. The building goals were always more specific in terms of content. Given the fact that each building was unique and each was beginning at a different starting point, holding each building accountable to the same increment of growth would be blatantly unfair.

ACTION PLANS

To reach higher performance levels and to change the status quo, action is required. Action must be thoughtful and based on the analytical results and diagnostic conclusions. For action to occur, the leadership team must be engaged in the process. For those actions to be successful, stakeholders must be involved either directly or indirectly.

As outgrowth of a thorough analysis and diagnosis, there is a plethora of issues requiring attention. The superintendent and the leadership team can assist and provide perspective as to what needs to be accomplished immediately and what other items can be deferred for action at a later time. One must also be cognizant that some action items may be longitudinal, requiring simultaneous *Action Plans* that involve immediate, short-term and long-term timelines.

After reviewing and verifying the results of a survey such as the *School Systems Cross-Check*, the superintendent and the leadership team may identify systemic elements for inclusion in a district plan. Alignment of the organization, building a culture of continuous improvement, creating a viable system of accountability, or improving the leadership capacity within the organization may necessitate systemic planning and action plans that may take several years to complete.

Building plans, on the other hand, are very specific to their identified goals and are developed internally by staff on an annual basis but also are subject to a review process. Effective plans are measurable and assign responsibility. While standardized assessments are recommended for local, state, national, and even global comparisons, building goals should rely on benchmarks and authentic assessments for charting progress throughout the school year.

A major challenge involves the execution of *Action Plans*. District office administrators and supervisors assist in the launching of action plans through data reviews, reports, and timelines for completion. Principals, as part of the building improvement team, monitor the actual execution of plans and hold those accountable for executing each step.

Previously, an example of district and building goals highlighted an attempt to improve the district and a school's reading performance. At the building level, a sub-goal expressed a target for improving the proficiency levels related to non-fiction content. An example of how *Action Plans* are generated for this goal at the district and building level is as follows:

DISTRICT ACTION PLAN

1) The superintendent and/or assistant superintendent will coordinate:

    - A Data Review with Building Improvement Teams;
    - Development of Building Triage Lists (see *Appendix A* #5);
    - Schedule and participate in quarterly reviews of data reports, benchmarks, and other indicators of success.

2) District team members facilitate a discussion on the correlation between standards, curriculum, benchmarks, and other assessments with building teams and departments.

3) Based on district needs, the district improvement team plans staff development directly related to goals and outcomes.

4) District team members facilitate the development of activities, exercises, and assignments associated with reading proficiency in the non-fiction area.

5) Curriculum supervisors develop strategies for integrating reading into all grade level curriculum programs.

BUILDING ACTION PLAN

1. Building Improvement Team will meet with the faculty to review the data and associated *Action Plan*.
2. Create an AM/PM reading support program.
3. Assign mentors for identified students on triage list.
4. Link standards, curriculum, and benchmarks to assessments.
5. Identify non-fiction titles for utilization at specific grade levels.
6. Create non-fiction passages and activities for utilization in the classroom.
7. Meet with grade and department level teachers to discuss strategies for the integration of reading into all classrooms.

BUILDING GOAL AND ACTION PLAN REVIEW PROCESS

Often overlooked in the improvement process is a formal review of a building's improvement plan involving its Goals, Actions Plans, Measurement Tools, and those assigned to monitor not only the overall plan but each action step within it. The review should include selected members of the leadership team, particularly instructional curriculum supervisors, the principal of the building, and a key member of the Building Improvement Team who coordinated its work.

While many would consider our review process formal, the review climate was very informal. In this setting, the principal would often negotiate the rate of growth for their school. Part of the negotiation involved a review of the "at-risk" students who were designated as "Not Proficient" on a standardized assessment and those that were considered "Marginally Proficient" which we defined as those students too close to the "cut off" line for proficiency.

Our initial discussion focused on how many "At-Risk" students could be effectively moved to proficiency or how many in the marginal area could be maintained. Realistically, there were potentially too many students in the "basic" range of proficiency which meant that moving all those students to proficiency in one year would be impossible. These students were never ignored because the interventions that were implemented also had the potential to impact their achievement as well.

The improvement discussions were structured to simply identify an appropriate expectation for growth in a particular building. Action Plans were always designed to improve performance levels for all students.

Other conversations focused on the quality of the Action Plan and attempted to determine the potential effectiveness of the plan. Each action step was discussed in terms of its viability to attain the designated outcome. Discussions involving what we termed "Triage" also took place.

"Triage" is a medical term for determining the extent of an injury and the prioritization of treatment options. In other words, in its application to schools, we wanted to ascertain which interventions were most effective regarding various student groups so as to move them closer to proficiency (see Appendix A #5). Student groups were often defined by those subgroups identified on standardized assessments.

The discussion was honest but integral to articulating a plan that was realistic and one that would move us closer to higher performance. After approving the building plan, the next step was to discuss each plan with each respective faculty and other stakeholders.

TRANSPARENCY

When the various review levels have been completed, it is only at that time that the entire plan for improvement should be disseminated. The superintendent should again discuss the district goals with the board but in this rendition, the superintendent should summarize how these goals were transferred to the *Building Improvement Team* for *Action Plan* development.

At the building level the stakeholders, who are integral in the development of the building plan, should take the lead in presenting the plan to the faculty and staff. While the building principal is an integral member of the *Building Improvement Team*, the building plan for improvement is generally more accepted when peers deliver the annual "marching orders." A message from peers is perceived as a more of a "grassroots" effort versus a top-down administrative directive.

Since these goals will become the driving force in the delivery of instruction to improve performance, leaders must be strategic about the communication of these goals to all stakeholders in the district. Throughout this process there have been ample opportunities to discuss how the improvement process will impact the organization's alignment, culture, accountability, and leadership roles, but further reporting is necessary to continue to build support for the instructional shifts that are inevitably necessary.

Not only should district goals be prominently displayed on the district website, continuous discussion and conversation in a variety of forums is necessary to adequately integrate the plan into every fabric of the organization and community. Opportunities abound to interview principals, curriculum supervisors, or teachers regarding aspects of the plan on cable television, newspaper releases, internet blogs, or podcasts.

In our case, it was difficult to have a conversation about instruction without invariably mentioning the initiative's acronym. The program became a sense of pride. It was immediately synonymous with our district and the success derived from it.

SUMMARY

- *District and School Improvement Teams* are key structures in the performance process.
- A building and district review process ensures consistency in the delivery of the performance plan.
- District goals transfer to the building level.
- Goals are specific, measurable, and customized to organizational levels.
- *Action Plans* operationalize goals.
- Transparency builds stakeholder support.

RECOMMENDATIONS

- Design a structure for delivering the performance improvement plan.
- Develop an approval/review process.
- Create a communications strategy for the finalized plan.
- Continue to build support by continuously utilizing all available media platforms.

ACTIVITIES

- Examine the alignment of resources, curriculum, and instruction to district/building goals and outcomes.
- Review a school or district's goal development.
- Examine the review process for goal and action plan approval.
- Review *Appendix A #5*: Triage List-Students.
- Complete *Appendix B #9*: Building and District Goals.

Chapter 8

Sustaining Performance

The large three-story, corner Victorian house weathered many cold winter nights. Yet, when the glow of the fire in the furnace began to wane, it became necessary to stoke its embers. No one really wanted to enter the basement in the middle of the night, but no one wanted to awaken in a cold home.

The big house had a coal furnace that required constant attention and monitoring. Complacency and neglect would result in an extinguished fire. On the other hand, nurturing and providing it with fuel would sustain it.

Igniting Performance is like a fire. It requires a steadfast commitment to all of its component parts to keep the plan for higher performance alive.

CONTINUOUS IMPROVEMENT OF PERFORMANCE

The mandate to seek excellence and to improve performance requires continuous improvement. It begins with an ingrained philosophy which continually refines the organizational structure and key elements within that structure that impact performance. It also strictly adheres to the performance principles and beliefs that continually guide the process of improvement. The process is not one of complacency but rather one that is continually responding to the internal and external factors that exert pressure on it, adjusting to them and maintaining a course of action that produces high performing outcomes.

Moreover, schools and school districts need "to identify people who know what to do, to develop the capacity of those in the organization to learn what to do, and to create settings in which people who know how to do, teach those who don't."[1] By doing so, schools and school districts can maintain a level of consistency in the implementation of the plan for improvement.

Linked to continuous improvement is the organization's ability to provide a professional development program that is aligned to the district's goals and one that eliminates those obstacles that are impeding performance. Professional development programs that upgrade teacher skills and delivery methods pay dividends in the long run. It keeps the stakeholders in the forefront of the delivery process to acquire engagement techniques that are motivational.

Another consideration in developing a professional development program is recognition that not all teachers have the same skill levels. A "one size fits all" professional development program may initially have merit when the goal is simply to provide a rudimentary orientation to a specific skill. When the complexity of the desired skill begins to unfold, acquisition of the required competencies may necessitate a structured learning program.

A differentiated, yet cohesive plan based on a practitioner's skill level, allows staff to begin at the appropriate level of competency and progress through various offerings to reach mastery. While more time-consuming and expensive, a differentiated program will ultimately prove more effective and empowering to those in the system.

Technology training offers the most poignant example of the range of faculty skill and competency. Such a range is illustrated below:

In an attempt to "get a handle" on the competency level of the staff, a survey was distributed to determine each teacher and administrator's skill level. The survey ranked skill level from basic to proficient on a number of platforms and teaching systems utilized in the classroom. It was no surprise that the results yielded a range of proficiency.

From the survey's results, we were able to design a differentiated training program for all skill levels over a number of semesters and years. A differentiated design was also replicated in all areas of instructional programming. Even though most faculty members eventually moved to a mastery level of proficiency, the basic level programs were maintained to some degree because there were always new employees that required it.

An often-overlooked nuance of professional development is the inclusion of administrators in the process. Logically, principals and supervisors who are tasked with the observation and supervision process should have the same level of competency regarding instructional programs as those staff members that they are evaluating.

If supervisors are perceived as competent in a specific skill, technology, or method, supervisory feedback is more likely to be accepted, especially when support is offered. In fact, when principals and supervisors receive instructional training, "76% of those observed stated that they received actionable feedback."[2]

Differentiated training, an induction program, implementing "cutting edge" methodology and pedagogy, along with a results-driven culture that is flexible enough to adjust to trends that are substantiated by data and research allow the organization to be continually rejuvenated and reenergized. Alignment of professional development to goals, action plans, and outcomes keeps the organization focused, efficient, and sustainable.

TEAMWORK

Without creating and supporting a culture of teamwork, the work which is necessary to sustain and improve performance in the schools and school districts would grind to a halt. Only through the collaborative and the collective efforts of focused professionals will the results of the organization improve. The work regardless of how innovative or effective when produced by working in "silos" or in isolation will realistically only benefit a small fraction of students.

To create a program that benefits ALL students, the administration and the faculty must come together to discuss what should be taught and how it should be taught. In such an environment, individual accolades are deferred for the betterment of the school and its students. Real synergy and growth are only sustainable as an outgrowth of teamwork.

In education we have many wonderful teachers and administrators but for a variety of reasons they withdraw from the collaborative process. It may be the result of frustration in dealing with confusing and failed initiatives or possibly just the instinct to survive in a chaotic, poorly organized environment. Under difficult circumstances, many teachers and administrators do the best that they can do.

Some teachers feel alone and yearn for the support of others who can assist them. Others recognize the difficulty in organizing the staff for collaboration. Synergy requires the efforts of administrators who believe in the value of teamwork and collaboration. It requires leaders who are willing to find the time in the teaching week for team planning, curriculum work, and the discussion of practices that have the greatest impact on students and instruction.

With support, time, and teamwork, the performance initiative can thrive rather than collapse under the weight of higher expectations and additional demands. Whenever instructional issues were discussed, teacher groups immediately wanted to know when time would be created in the day for the group to work together. For effective collaboration to occur, we created common planning time and provided other options such as release time. It required a reallocation of resources to make it a reality but was well worth the effort and expenditure.

Teams have the ability to disperse demands or delegate to those in the group. Teams have the ability to bend with pressure but not break.

A synergistic team, when confronted with adversity, recognizes the need to pull together rather than bemoan the obvious. Such a team finds creative solutions to the problems associated with time and mandates.

For the most part, schools have everything that they need to achieve. It is a matter of organizing its component parts to reach a level of synergy for progress to emerge. Eliminating the disconnections between Alignment, Attitude, and Accountability is essential. Having the Adept Leadership to do it and sustain is critical.

Individuals do make a difference but the real power of growth lies in the team. It is through the "power of team" that real solutions are devised and goals are met. When the team meets, reviews progress, adjusts its direction, and charts new action plans for the future, it is then that the team breathes new life into performance process.

COLLECTIVE RECOGNITION

Consistent with shared responsibility, collaboration, and teamwork is the belief that recognition for improvement should be shared by the group. To further sustain the performance process, the development of a system which rewards meeting a school's goals is encouraged. In this system the entire staff of a building shares in the award. The superintendent who oversees the entire improvement process, upon reviewing the measurable goals for a building, determines whether they have been met.

In our district, we designed a system with monetary rewards based on meeting a Building's Goals. Each building had a reading and a math goal. A separate award was made for meeting each goal. As part of the plan, a formula, which factored a building's enrollment into the reward equation, provided a "per pupil" award by varying the amount of money that each building could earn. If successful, a monetary award was made to the specific Building School Improvement Team. The monetary reward was then utilized for the purchase of school-related materials, equipment, or a program that would further benefit the performance initiative.

A safeguard was also built into the reward process. If a building did not meet either goal, a base amount was still allocated to the school. There were those who argued that the safeguard would diminish the significance of those buildings that met their goals, but it was instituted so that the failing school would have the resources available to the team to assist them with future planning.

The base award did not replicate those funds awarded to the successful schools but rather was considered a "hand up" to the failing school and to proactively counter any potential morale issue in the failing school. At the same time, it provided the motivation to succeed in successive years.

The program for collective recognition not only empowered the staff, but it reinforced support for the process. Each year the rewards provided a "jump start" for years to follow.

TEACHER LEADERSHIP

"Within every school or district there is a sleeping giant of teacher leadership which can be a strong catalyst for change. By using the energy of teachers as agents of school change, the reform of public education will stand a better chance of building momentum."[3] In fact, these internal stakeholders are one of the key ingredients to not only launching a performance plan for improvement but sustaining it as well. "Teachers who choose the path of leadership become owners and investors in their schools, rather than mere tenants."[4]

Teachers who choose to become teacher leaders actually become key members of the leadership team who can assist in creating more authenticity in teaching and assessment practices. These teacher leaders not only have an opportunity to confront barriers in a school's culture and structure but actually can translate ideas and solutions into systems of action. Clearly, these internal leaders can provide a perspective from a teacher's lens, challenge existing teacher beliefs, and provide support around the "big picture" of improving performance.

Most often, teacher leadership is associated with *Coaching* and *Mentoring* programs. Even the most effective schools and school districts cannot assume that the instructional staff has the capability to access standard-driven resources and materials or effectively assess and evaluate student progress and then differentiate instruction. These areas of instruction are difficult for even the most seasoned staff members let alone a novice in the field. Each may need support.

Teacher leaders can also be designated as a member of a *Building Improvement Team*, write curriculum, act as a demonstration teacher, plan and deliver professional development programs, serve as a member of an intervention team, or become a *Master Teacher* (see *Appendix A #3*).

Selecting teachers who were masters of their craft was always a challenge. The criteria were designed to be rigorous and the selection required flawless execution. Along the way, tough and sometimes unpopular decisions had to be made. In the end we needed to select models of teaching that everyone could endorse.

The application process involved and required the endorsement of the principal along with documenting several years of teacher leadership within a building and of course, outstanding observation reports. Each teacher applicant was observed by a team that consisted of a non-nominating principal, supervisor, and other teacher peers. The team's reports were forwarded to the superintendent who made the final selection.

The politics of selecting an effective teacher versus a well-liked teacher was a high stakes decision. We had to "get it right." Failure to do so would undermine the program.

While it was important to publicize the final decision, it was more significant internally to identify the teacher's instructional expertise and strengths. Some of the teachers instructed coaches, others wrote curriculum while still others participated in the delivery of professional development programs. We were utilizing the hidden talent that was always there. Now, they were part of the team to improve performance and to sustain the process. The program endorsed our belief in empowerment as well as our belief that excellence matters.

PROMOTING PERFORMANCE

A cognizant effort is necessary to continually generate excitement around the plan and its execution. The journey to higher performance is an exhausting one. It is easy for administrators and teachers to tire of high expectations and increasing demands. Recognition of all efforts in the execution of the plan is essential in maintaining the momentum. Off-setting any form of misinterpretation, misrepresentation, or attempts to undermine the plan is critical to sustaining it.

When a school or school district invests in professional development and endorses a shared decision-making model with shared responsibility for outcomes, the performance plan is supported by its internal stakeholders and is insulated from fluctuations of perception or criticism from external stakeholders.

In schools and districts, there is always a new group of stakeholders that is cycling through the organization. There are parents or newly elected board members and even emerging "self-anointed" community activists. Each individual or group generally has a preconceived idea about the school or district, how effective it is, or what it should be teaching. Often, many of these ideas are rooted in personal experiences when they attended school and how they were educated. Some of these individuals wanted the school district to outright adopt an idea that they were advocating.

Whether they attended a committee meeting, regular board meeting, or appeared at a parent forum, our best advocates for a school or district's direction or practice are those empowered by it. When testimonials are part of narrative that involves a well-conceived plan with a "track record" of success, it is a difficult target to attack.

Sometimes, a simple explanation would be enough for a detractor. Other times, it required a personal meeting with support staff, and sometimes it involved an explanation of the data and the research. Remember, you have a right to your opinion but not the facts. Once a stakeholder leader, board member, teacher, parent, or child has experienced the result of improved performance, it reinforces and sustains the initiative. There is no substitute for demonstrated success.

Despite such success, every opportunity should be made to continually promote the plan as well as those executing it. Whenever possible, data which tracks the growth of buildings or the students should be provided. All stakeholders at any given time should understand how the district or individual school is progressing.

In a performance driven district, there should be no hidden agendas. Transparency builds trust, promotes understanding, and insulates the school or district from needless distractions or inadvertent changes of direction.

MONITORING GROWTH

Critical to sustaining growth is the development of a system which monitors all aspects of the performance plan. While there are state standardized test scores to track each student and building, local benchmarks and authentically designed assessments are valuable in monitoring weekly or monthly student progress in the classroom. Developing such a system of monitoring requires an understanding of the content in a standardized assessment as well as the curriculum which should align with it.

Building benchmarks and classroom assessments at the local level also require an alignment to the overarching standardized assessments. This type of alignment provides a base standard. Any school or district can choose to exceed such a standard design. It is only through this type of design and accountability that a district will succeed and maintain its sustainability as a high performing district.

Beyond the data reviews, it is essential to monitor the effectiveness of the curriculum and the methodology. Understanding the curriculum and the methodology allows principals, supervisors, coaches, and mentors to provide accurate feedback to those in the classroom. This process is further supported when the classroom observers receive training to understand the observational criteria from which evaluations are developed. Consistency in the observation and supervision process across the district maintains high expectations and district focus.

Complicating the issue of linking performance to accountability is the utilization of generic rubrics purchased from educational publishing houses.

If performance is to grow in a dramatic manner, the observational rubric should reflect the goals and outcomes of the organization along with the identified methodology and pedagogy necessary to do so. Generic rubrics can be infused with "grassroots" initiatives, which elevate the credibility of the instrument to practitioners in the field.

Monitoring and accountability are often viewed as a slippery slope by educators. Too many professionals view the monitoring of growth as punitive, selective, or restrictive. Finding the right balance between monitoring, accountability, and support is critical. While there is inherent anxiety within every system of accountability and its supervisory process, the process must be viewed primarily as one that helps all members of the organization to grow. At the same time, it must also move the organization toward reaching its goals by assisting in the execution of the performance plan.

If monitoring and supervision are implemented in a manner that is supportive, builds the capacity of the individual, and attempts to find viable solutions to problems, staff members will embrace it. Leadership is more than pushing, pronouncing, and demanding. It includes modeling.

Coaching and *Mentoring* are excellent examples of how to move a school and district in a positive direction without turmoil. Staff members are more willing to accept feedback from other less threatening peers.

When *District* and *Building Teams* utilize data to identify disconnections and identify solutions, the results can be dramatic. When the organization is aligned and the entire staff is accountable for its outcomes, the growth can be exponential. Without measurement against a standard or goal, the organization will drift aimlessly and without purpose.

Every facet of the school or district requires monitoring through designated indicators and outcomes. It is only through this monitoring process that the success or failure of the school or district's initiatives can be determined. Without establishing the requisite baseline data, an organization will never ascertain its progress on a continuum of higher performance.

SUMMARY

- To sustain performance, key concepts must be embedded into the organization.
- The six concepts necessary for sustaining performance are as follows:
  - Continuous improvement
  - Teamwork
  - Collective recognition
  - Teacher leadership
  - Promoting performance
  - Monitoring growth

RECOMMENDATIONS

- Commit to a system of continuous improvement.
- Foster teamwork.
- Recognize group and individual accomplishments.
- Empower teacher leaders.
- Increase awareness of performance initiatives and district progress.
- Develop a system of accountability that is inclusive, supportive, and shared.

ACTIVITIES

- Review *Appendix A* #3: Master Teacher.
- Conduct a survey of faculty proficiency on an instructional skill.
- Review *Appendix A* #4: Observation/Stratification List.

Chapter 9

Case Studies

CASE STUDY #1

Background

It was an underachieving district. For years, the board of directors invested heavily in the district with the hope that it would "turn the corner" and become a bastion of achievement for the region. The parents recognized the importance of an education and the implications of not being a top tier district.

The administration responded to board pressure by seeking programs that might provide the necessary "jump start" that the board was seeking. Program after program was purchased and layered on previous programs but nothing seemed to spark any semblance of growth. In frustration the board turned its "ire" on its teachers and its staff.

First, the board of directors sought the assistance of a prestigious university which suggested the implementation of a merit pay plan. Second, upon the suggestion of its solicitor, the plan was incorporated into the district's negotiated teacher's contract. The integration of the plan stalled negotiations for years but was later mandated as part of a binding arbitration agreement. The plan involved a complicated 26 factor formula that when calculated would yield the best performing teachers in the district.

Needless to say, the teachers were not thrilled with the plan, the $500 bonus or the selections that the formula produced. The community and parents were highly skeptical and dubious about the selections. There was dissension on the board but all wanted a solution that could produce improved student outcomes.

The skepticism, dissension, and outright anger rolled into the next contract negotiations. Teachers demanded the removal of the plan. The board wanted to "save face" and the parents were caught in the middle.

As an outgrowth of the negotiations, all parties agreed to participate in a collaborative plan to improve instruction. The plan involved *District and Building Goals* and *Master Teacher* recognition. An integral part of the plan was a system of "checks and balances" in the sharing of power along with an emphasis on connecting curriculum and instruction to a system of accountability. In essence, the district was embarking on a plan to improve performance that was systemic.

From the outset, it was clear that the district had the internal capability to improve and the potential to leap forward toward improving its performance. It was simply a matter of its alignment, culture, system of accountability, and leadership.

Groundwork

Since there was a consensus to improve, it was necessary to clearly explain how the district was going to shift philosophically. Developing an understanding of the philosophical tenets was essential in changing the culture. These tenets were as follows:

- All students can learn.
- Each school controls enough variables to assure that all children can learn.
- A school's stakeholders are the most qualified individuals to implement the needed changes.
- There are several kinds of schools in the United States—improving schools, status quo schools, and declining schools.
- Every school can improve.
- The capacity to improve your school resides in your school right now.
- All students in the school are important.
- Change is a process, not an event.
- Existing people are the best change elements.

Some of the steps included tenets from research conducted by the American Society for Quality's (ASQ) Koalaty Kid Program,[1] the Effective Schools[2] movement, and others.

The framework which operationalized these tenets specifically focused on student achievement, student learning, and performance. The model paid simultaneous attention to issues of quality and equity. The district recognized the importance of providing an explanation to faculty and staff that the model, which utilizes *Building and District Goals*, is collaborative in form by recognizing that improving a school requires the cooperation of all stakeholders—board members, administrators, teachers, support staff, and parents. Stakeholders had to believe in the mission, core values, and be willing to take action that would lead to success.

Additionally, for the initiative to be successful, the school district had to adhere to the following guiding concepts:

- Research Based
- Data Driven
- Student Performance Focused
- Quality and Equity
- Transparency
- Collaboration
- Curriculum Focus
- Best Practice Methodology
- Systemic
- Sustainable: Organizationally and Financially

The district also recognized that the entire process was going to involve multiple steps. Some of these steps included:

- Developing a district vision and belief system.
- Aligning the curriculum with national and state standards.
- Creating a system of assessment.
- Developing a focused staff development program.
- Raising the expectations for learning for all students.
- Reviewing policies and procedures for their impact on achievement.
- Creating an atmosphere of pride and responsibility.
- Creating an environment of continuous improvement and learning.

Moving forward, it became apparent that the district had to assess its current status through the utilization of data, obtaining formal and informal feedback and validating the responses. With concrete data and valid feedback, the district was then positioned to develop a plan for improvement. In this case, it was important to integrate beliefs and implementation steps into an existing strategic plan so that there was alignment.

To maximize student performance, it was determined that curriculum, instruction, testing, and grading along with outcomes and standards must incorporate the components of accountability for real progress to occur. Each of these areas had clearly defined indicators for success by identifying those responsible for delivering them.

Aspirations

Every school district has an image of itself. It may or may not be accurate. All schools and districts also have an idea of what they can accomplish. The challenge is to align its aspirations with a workable plan that actually produces tangible results.

In this case, stakeholders wanted to not only reach for excellence but to be among the best. In the effort to reach a high level of performance, the plan focused on student achievement and teaching excellence. There was also a desire to restore a deep sense of pride, which was missing for years, in the district.

To become a high-performing district, it is critical to stretch beyond local expectations in the formulation of high-level targets for success. For stakeholders it was important to be among the best at the state and regional level.

The delineated aspirations were daunting and the implications for change at all levels of the organization were significant. Those aspirations were as follows:

- Produce highly competitive SAT and state standardized test scores.
- Increase the number of Merit Scholars.
- Increase scholarship awards.
- Increase the number of graduating students that attend highly desirable universities.
- Reduce the achievement gap between the general population and the disaggregate groups.

Having been devastated by student transfers or parents not enrolling children in the district due to the large number of private schools in proximity to its boundaries, it was also essential to attract the number of those students who have private school as an option. Class size had to be limited for the district to become an attractive option. Of course, the program at all levels had to become even more challenging.

Stakeholders also recognized the importance of empowering teachers and highlighting excellence in the execution of a plan to improve performance. A seamless component of the culture had to include K–12 teacher collaboration. Professional development for teachers and the leadership team had to mirror or exceed national standards for excellence.

MULTI-YEAR INSTRUCTIONAL IMPROVEMENT PLAN K–12

Item 1. Mission Statement

The mission of the school district was to graduate citizens who are able and committed to fulfilling their potential and maximizing their contribution to society. The school district would achieve its mission by working in partnership with the community to:

- provide learning experiences which instill common societal values.
- develop critical thinking skills.
- encourage the development and application of knowledge.
- value human diversity.
- prepare a generation of life-long learners to inherit and lead our complex society.

Item 2. Educational and Organizational Goals

The plan specified the following eight district-wide Educational and Organizational Goals:

- develop a district vision and belief system that focuses on student achievement.
- align curriculum with standards.
- create a system of assessment.
- develop a focused staff development program.
- raise expectations for learning for students.
- review policies and procedures as they impact student achievement.
- create an atmosphere of pride and responsibility.
- create an environment of continuous professional improvement.

A multi-year plan to achieve these goals was as follows:

Year 1

By the conclusion of year 1, the school district will increase the district-wide standardized test scores on the reading and the writing portion of the state's standardized assessment to the 85th percentile or above. Mathematics scores on the state assessment will also increase to the 85th percentile. Overall, SAT scores will increase by 16 points or within the 1020 range.

Year 2

At the conclusion of year 2, reading and mathematics scores will increase to the 90th percentile on the state's standardized assessment. The SAT scores will improve by 30 points to the 1050+ range resulting in the district placing in the top one-third of the region.

Adjustments in programming through the implementation of the following initiatives in the first year were required as follows:

- Effective Schools Orientation
- Language Arts and Mathematics Curricula Alignment (K-6)
- Revision of Vocabulary and Spelling Lists (K-5)
- Pilot Mathematics Revisions (6–8)
- SAT Pilot Program
- Update Data Management System
- Develop Recommendations for Full-Time Kindergarten
- Create Criteria Referenced Exams
- Implement Summer Reading Programs

Program adjustments in year two were as follows:

- Language Arts and Curriculum Alignment (7–12)
- Implement Benchmark Assessments
- Implement 6–8 Math Revision
- Update Data Management System Implementation
- Lesson Plan/Observational Revision to Reflect Changes in Curriculum and Higher Expectations
- Instructional Model Development
- SAT Revisions Complete
- Complete Kindergarten Revisions
- Implement Benchmark Assessments (7–12)
- Schedule Extended Program Reviews for Sciences and Humanities

Item 3. Academic Standards for Student Achievement

Over the next six years, the district further aligned its curriculum, instruction, and assessment programs in the following subject areas:

- Social Studies
- Arts and Humanities
- Career and Vocational Education
- World Languages
- Health, Safety, and Physical Education
- Family and Consumer Education
- Technology Education

Item 4. Assessment Plan

The district decided to continue its use of multiple sources of data and assessment tools to measure knowledge and skills possessed by students, which were aligned with standards. The plan's goal was to include national and state assessments, criterion referenced tests and district developed performance-oriented assessments. To develop this system of assessment, the following steps were required:

Step 1. Initially the district established Assessment Committees for policy review, data collection and analysis, input and utilization via data management warehousing/data mining, assessment results, applications to curricular/instructional decisions, and the reporting of results. Committees were composed of central office administrators, curriculum supervisors, staff developers, curriculum/resource support teachers, principals, board members, community representatives, and parents.

Cross-grade level committees also designed an assessment plan for individual students, classes, grades, cohorts, and schools. District profiles which included assessments that highlighted and tracked student performance and progress over time toward the meeting of standards were developed.

The specific responsibilities of the cross-grade level committees which included making decisions about assessments included:

- analyzing assessment data/tools and identifying gaps.
- making assessment decisions regarding evidence of connecting proficiency to standards.
- determining if assessments are aligned with state and local standards.
- making accountability decisions.
- reviewing district policy related to assessment and forwarding recommendations to the superintendent and the board of directors.
- verifying rubrics and anchor papers.
- making recommendations to the Professional Education Committee to assure adequate staff development is available to equip staff with appropriate assessment skills.
- determining dates for implementing and institutionalizing district assessments.
- identifying units of performance, accountability, and reporting systems.
- developing a calendar for field testing and revising assessments.

Step 2. Develop procedures to systematically gather district, state, and national assessment data.

Step 3. Coordinate the development of standards and methods of student achievement (assessment tools) required to assist students who have not demonstrated the attainment of academic standards at a proficient or higher level.

Step 4. Specify and implement policies and dissemination procedures, including mailings, newsletters, websites, community newspapers, public meetings, and individual consultations for providing assessment results to students, parents, and the public.

In essence, the district utilized the following methods and measures to determine progress toward the standards:

- District and Grade Level Assessment Tools
  - District-Wide End of Course/Unit Exams
  - Qualitative Reading Inventories
  - "Running Records"
  - Performance Tasks
- State Standardized Assessments (Reading, Math, Writing, Science)
- National Standardized Assessments
  - SAT
  - Advanced Placement
  - ACT

Item 5. Student Achievement Improvement Plans

Each year the district planned to conduct an analysis of district data from its various assessment tools to guide and improve curriculum and instruction. This analysis included a review of the "hard data" from district, state, and classroom assessments. Although each assessment yielded different data, the district recognized the importance of reviewing this data and developing an overview so as to understand strengths and weaknesses of students and the district. The review process followed the following procedures:

- District central office personnel gathered and charted data from each grade level.
- Using the district expectancy level per standard area, central office personnel noted results that were above or below proficiency levels.
- The above two steps were repeated by utilizing building level data with the School Improvement Team. Principals and teachers utilized this data to review performance against building goals and to compare and contrast it with district data.
- Each School Improvement Team selected improvement goals for the succeeding year and identified individual students in need of support.
- District support staff and subject area curriculum staff assisted teachers in locating support materials and research to further support techniques ("best practices") to enhance the instructional program in goal areas.

- District support staff and subject curriculum staff produced classroom tools to assist teachers in monitoring student progress toward proficiency on the standards in the selected goal areas.
- The assessment committee also reviewed attendance records and allocation of instructional time in each standard area for potential problems.

As part of the plan, School Improvement Planning was decentralized at the building level but improvement efforts were coordinated through the District Improvement Team to foster consistency in the areas such as Staff Development, Instructional Material Selection, and Technology applications.

In addition to the aforementioned processes, the district routinely engaged in the following activities:

- Utilization of district-wide rubrics for all grade levels
- Provided on-going professional development education opportunities to all teachers on standards, methodology, and technology
- Participated in a consortium with other districts on topics involving teaching and learning
- Created an interactive website for standards, assessment, and teacher resources
- Provided direct reading instruction for all K–12 teachers
- Utilized teaching strategies to encourage higher level thinking and problem-solving skills
- Provided multiple opportunities for students to engage in open-ended tasks in all content areas
- Reviewed school district results and modified the district's curriculum accordingly
- Participated in state field testing

Item 6. Plan for Additional Instructional Opportunities

The district designed various programs to assist those students who are experiencing difficulty in achieving the targeted academic standards. To effect the positive changes in the achievement of students who did not meet or were identified as minimally proficient, the following services were provided by organizational level:

Elementary

- Reading and Math Curriculum Resource Teachers
- Strategic Tutoring Achievers Results (STAR)—After-School Tutoring
- Child Study and Instructional Support Teams
- FAST—Evening Guidance Program for "at risk" Families

- Homework Club—Weekly Tutoring
- Mentoring
- Technology Assistance
- High School Tutoring
- Parental Academic Forum for Parent Assistance with Curriculum and Homework Assignments

Middle School

- Reading and Math Curriculum Resource Teachers
- PASS—After-School Tutoring for Those Students Scoring at the Basic Level
- Mandatory Activity Period—Scheduled for Students Failing Academically
- Transitional Math and English classes
- CARE—Teachers Provided Tutoring and Homework Assistance
- Individual Tutoring
- Mentoring
- Technology Assistance
- Standardized Test Preparation during Student Activity Periods

High School

- Reading for Young Adults
- Reading across Content Areas
- Reading and Math Resource Teachers

Many initiatives and steps in the plan were implemented over several years. Within five years, the district met its goal of becoming a state and regional leader.

CASE STUDY #2

Background

It was a very small school district in the Midwest that could not move one student into the proficient range on the state's standardized assessment. Despite small class sizes and a tight-knit community with strong local control over its program, the school district appeared to wander the educational landscape for solutions. Annually, the school district purchased new programs in its attempt to improve achievement. Unfortunately, nothing seemed to work.

After attending our presentation at a professional conference in Boston, Massachusetts, a member of the district's School Board of Directors reached out to our consultant team with the hope that we could reverse the district's trend of unsatisfactory achievement. They were surprised that we accepted the challenge.

Status Assessment

Prior to an on-site visitation, an extensive list of documents such as the district's strategic plan, instructional goals, student achievement reports, state assessment data, and board policies were requested for our review. We wanted to become very familiar with how the instructional program was delivered and to determine what was important to them, at least on paper.

We also requested that each teacher and administrative team member complete the *School Systems Cross-Check*. Our goal was to identify disconnections within the organization associated with its Alignment, Culture/Atmosphere, Accountability, and Leadership. Responses from each group were reviewed and later verified through group interviews with key personnel. When the verified responses were also considered in the context of the document review, a picture of the district's focus began to emerge.

The *School Systems Cross-Check* administered to both teachers and administrators attempted to pinpoint the perception of each group as to the district's effectiveness in key areas that impact instruction and achievement. Each group was requested to rank item effectiveness in terms of highly effective, moderately effective, or low effectiveness. The ranking of key instructional elements critical in improving performance by teachers and administrators is illustrated below.

(For clarity, administrators were defined as the superintendent, principals, and the district's leadership team which included curriculum supervisors or department heads.)

Teacher perceptions indicated a larger number of elements that contribute to a school or district's effectiveness in the moderate to low rating range. Only a few items in the area of accountability were considered highly effective.

Conversely, the table of administrative perceptions was heavily skewed toward the high or moderately effective range. Few items were ranked by the administration as low and those items that were ranked low tended to target areas associated with teacher performance such as teaching skills, buy-in, professional development, and parental involvement.

The administrative perceptions of key elements in an effective school or district are listed as follows:

Cross-Check Matrix Analysis: Teacher Perceptions

Alignment

High	Moderate	Low
	Philosophy	Strategic Plan
	Assessments	Goals
	Programs	Solutions
		Expectations
		Focus
		Indicators
		Empowerment
		Communication
		Effective Solutions
		Integrated Values

Achievement-Focused Attitude

High	Moderate	Low
	Staff Strengths	Demonstrated Values
	Working toward Goals	Adequate Time
	Collaboration	Encouraging
		Teacher Leadership
		Recognition
		Utilizing Teacher Skills
		Buy-In
		Mentoring
		Professional Development

Accountability

High	Moderate	Low
Assessment	Data Utilization	Evaluation Linkage
Goal Design	Collective Design	Motivation
Expectations	Action Plans	Staff Support
Goal Measurement	Classroom Goals	Measurement Skills
		Outcomes
		Individual Accountability

Adept Leadership

High	Moderate	Low
	Goal Review Process	Assumes Responsibility
	Resources	Eliminates Distractions
	Execution	Focus
		Practicality
		Flexibility
		Inclusiveness
		Risk Taking
		Stakeholders
		Fair/Equitable
		Teamwork
		Values

Cross-Check Matrix Analysis: Teacher Perceptions

	Adept Leadership	
High	Moderate	Low
		Grows People
		Models
		Assumes Responsibility
		Expertise
		Creates Learning Environment
		Communicates
		Recognition
		Parents/Community

Cross-Check Matrix Analysis: Administrative Responses (Cross-Referenced Teacher Responses in Parentheses)*

	Alignment	
High	Moderate	Low
Strategic Plan (L)	Communication (L)	Integrated Values (L)
Goals (L)	Effective Solutions (M)	
Philosophy (M)	Inclusive (M)	
Assessments (M)		
Solutions (L)		
Programs (M)		
Expectations (L)		
Focus (L)		
Indicators (L)		
Empowering (L)		

	Achievement-Focused Attitude	
High	Moderate	Low
Demonstrated Values (L)	Staff Strengths (M)	Teacher Skills (L)
Collaboration (M)	Working toward Goals (M)	Buy-In (L)
Adequate Time (L)		Mentoring (L)
Encouraging (L)		Professional Development (L)
Teacher Leadership (L)		
Recognition (L)		

	Accountability	
High	Moderate	Low
Assessments (H)	Collective Design (M)	Outcomes (L)
Goal Design (H)	Motivation (L)	Individual Accountability (L)
Expectations (H)	Action Plans (M)	Curriculum Linkage (M)
Goals Measurement (H)	Classroom Goals (M)	Action Research (L)
Data Utilization (M)	Staff Support (L)	Data Warehouse (L)
Evaluation Linkage (L)	Measurement Proficiency (L)	

(Continued)

(Continued)

Cross-Check Matrix Analysis: Administrative Responses (Cross-Referenced Teacher Responses in Parentheses)*

Adept Leadership		
High	Moderate	Low
Proactive (L)	Goal Review (M)	
Parents/Community (L)	Communicates (L)	
Eliminates Distractions (L)	Execution (M)	
Focused (L)	Recognition (L)	
Practical (L)		
Flexible (L)		
Inclusion (M)		
Risk Taking (L)		
Stakeholders (L)		
Fair/Equitable (L)		
Resources (M)		
Teamwork (L)		
Values People (L)		
Grows People (L)		
Models (L)		
Assumes Responsibility (L)		
Expertise (L)		
Creates Environment (L)		

* While the perceptions above are those of the administrative team, the ranking in parentheses cross-references the responses of the teachers and highlights the disparity between the groups. [(H-High), (M-Moderate), (L-Low), Exemplary Schools Organization]

Overview

In essence the disparity between the groups highlights the disconnections in the organization and the possible dysfunction that can result from such disparities. Obviously, the data from the *School Systems Cross-Check* confirms that the administration and the teaching corps were on different pages almost entirely. It is not usual in such surveys for discrepancies to occur but the follow-up group interviews confirmed our suspicions as highlighted through the administration of the *School Systems Cross-Check* instrument.

The document analysis further revealed confusion regarding district and school instructional goals in that there were no less than three sets of different instructional priorities for the year. The journey forward had to begin with an Alignment of the organization to specific and measurable goals and outcomes which were understood by every member of the organization as a priority.

Setting instructional priorities had to involve the collaboration of the entire staff versus a top-down "command and control" initiative. Once the issue of Alignment was resolved, the other instructional links of Accountability and Leadership did fall into place. Certainly, creating an Atmosphere which included all stakeholders in the planning process did launch the district in the direction of continuous improvement.

In this particular case, it took an instructional crisis to recognize that the district possessed the internal capacity to resolve its issues. It was a matter of "getting through the instructional fog" and working with a set of principles to move the organization on a path toward higher performance outcomes.

SUMMARY

- Each case highlights the importance of creating a culture that focuses on instructional improvement, stakeholder inclusion, and the internal capacity to improve.
- The case studies illustrate the importance of utilizing a framework that generates collaboratively developed goals based on student achievement data and other supporting information.
- Schools and districts need to adhere to guiding principles and concepts in the implementation of a plan to improve performance.
- Leaders ascertain the aspirations/outcomes that stakeholders desire.

RECOMMENDATIONS

- Utilize a diagnostic and prescriptive framework which generates a plan with *School and District Goals* along with *Action Plans* for implementation.
- Keep the entire process transparent.
- Link the instructional plan to the key elements of Alignment, Atmosphere/ Culture, Accountability, and Leadership.
- Utilize the School Systems Cross-Check to identify disconnections for remediation.
- Utilize the *Hierarchy for School Development* to assist in the defining aspirations.

ACTIVITIES

- Complete *Appendix B* #10: Case Study Analysis

Conclusion

The issue of failing or underperforming schools in the United States is a very perplexing one, particularly in the context of funding, resources, and effort expended. Educational reformers have called for greater accountability in the classroom, more funding, improved teacher training and an assortment of other programs and initiatives.

Legislators have exerted pressure on the schools and school districts through a variety of mandates and "quick fix" solutions. The Department of Education has promoted incentive-based programs such as "Race to the Top" or Title I to stimulate performance. Despite these programs, overall growth on student achievement measures has remained negligible.

With significant local, state, and federal investment along with external pressure to improve, the question remains as to why educational leaders are not making significant gains in reading, math, and science and why other countries have been able to surpass U.S. achievement levels. Once one of the most admired institutions in the world, U.S. schools achieve at approximately the same level of many underdeveloped countries.

Researchers have been quick to conclude that our diverse demographics and the current influx of immigrants into the United States have compounded attempts to improve the schools and may have actually suppressed the real growth that has been taking place. Other researchers have focused on the impact of poverty, transiency, language proficiency, and a myriad of socioeconomic factors that inhibit school and school district performance.

While there is an abundance of data that points to the significant impact of poverty and other related factors on achievement levels, there is also significant evidence of schools which have excelled despite having a student body that is categorized as low socioeconomic, minority, and/or ethnically diverse. At the same time, there are highly resourced schools which struggle or underachieve.

Personal experience in both impoverished and underachieving well-financed schools has shaped a belief that all schools and school districts can improve performance and actually excel. Often, school and district leaders express support for an instructionally based agenda, but in reality, there is little substance or support from those leaders that define a commitment to their school or district as one of attaining excellence.

Too many leaders define instructional commitment or excellence through new programs, equipment, technology, or a "state of the art" building rather than the quality of the curriculum, teacher quality, methodology, and most importantly, how it all fits together.

Unfortunately, countless numbers of stakeholders (board members, superintendents, principals, teachers, and parents) have expressed in frustration "that it is what it is." Others have indicated that the leaders are either overwhelmed, don't really focus on instruction, or emphasize the "wrong things." Still others have described an atmosphere that is chaotic. They just "hunker down," close the door, and do what they know in order to survive.

If we are going to make our schools more academically competitive and even return to a position of worldwide educational prominence, a systemic improvement approach which involves all stakeholders is necessary. Just maintaining a status quo philosophy of "good enough" is not "good enough." Clearly, retreating to a survival mode or a blatant acceptance of "the way things are" is not acceptable.

Igniting School Performance was written to inspire stakeholders to coalesce around a plan to improve performance and provide stakeholders with tools that will assist in the planning process. Leaders are provided with strategies that will assist them in having all stakeholders embrace a performance-based agenda and the principles to drive such an agenda. Case studies concretely demonstrate how to move an organization forward toward excellence.

High performance is not just a dream but a conscious effort that is continuous, collaborative, inclusive, and rewarding. *Igniting School Performance* will give stakeholders the confidence to begin the journey toward higher performance and the "will" to succeed. It recognizes the importance of striving for perfection. It insists that we are not encumbered by the past but rather seeks new pathways which will enlighten and stimulate growth.

While it is preferred that the educational leader of a school or district assume responsibility for initiating the change process, the journey can be initiated by any stakeholder who recognizes that the status quo is no longer acceptable. It can simply begin at a board or a faculty meeting and even at a parent forum with a simple statement: *We need to change. We cannot continue to keep working in the same way and expect a different result.* Pressure from both internal and external stakeholders can effectively nudge a school or district to change.

If you are not continually improving as a school or district, you are falling behind due to the ever-evolving demands for highly qualified graduates in a highly competitive world. For a failing or underachieving school or district, the time is now. Thousands, if not millions of students, each year are ill-equipped for a world in which creativity, inferential thinking, abstract reasoning, problem-solving skills, and adaptability are highly desirable.

In essence, stakeholders control the destiny of students in their school or district. Let's begin the journey toward higher performance today. Let's *Ignite School Performance* so that ALL students cannot only succeed but thrive in a performance-focused school or district. Let's ignite the excellence that is embedded in the equity of learning for ALL students and to ignite the power of education which will propel our democracy forward as a beacon of performance, social mobility, and economic stability.

Part IV
APPENDICES

Appendix A:
Performance Instruments and Tools

A #1 SCHOOL SYSTEMS "CROSS CHECK": EVALUATION INSTRUMENT (REVISED EDITION 2019)

BACKGROUND

The School Systems "Cross Check" examines the interconnection of school and district processes and programs by "cross checking" embedded performance threads in key organizational areas.

The key elements and organizational threads which are examined in the "Cross Check" instrument include the following:

- Alignment
- Atmosphere/Attitude or Culture
- Accountability
- Adept Leadership

Systems "Cross Check" attempts to research an organization for the existence key elemental threads by identifying tangible, concrete demonstrations of those threads and to provide a framework for which to make recommendations that will result in a more effective organization.

DIRECTIONS

Rank responses to the questions in each of the four areas (Alignment, Atmosphere/Attitude, Accountability, and Adept Leadership) as High (3), Moderate (2). or Low (1). For example:

- a High ranking (3) indicates a high prevalence, presence, or existence of a *characteristic or term* identified in the question;
- a Moderate ranking (2) indicates a moderate prevalence, presence, or existence of a *characteristic or term* identified in the question;
- a Low ranking (1) indicates little existence or presence of the identified *characteristic or term* in the question.

DEFINITIONS

Student Achievement (SA) refers to student performance in academic and instructional areas.

Leadership involves the superintendent, principal, assistant principals, supervisors, and others identified as school administrators or configured leadership teams.

ALIGNMENT

Focus: All practices, processes, and goals are aligned from the "boardroom" to the classroom.

1. The district utilizes a *comprehensive instructional plan* as a framework in the development of the organization's goals. 1–2–3.
2. The district conducts an *annual review* of existing programs for effectiveness. 1–2–3.
3. The district developed *measurable goals* with timelines for completion. 1–2–3.
4. Annual *district goals are aligned* with building goals. 1–2–3.
5. The district's *values, mission, and vision match behaviors* exhibited by its members. 1–2–3.
6. The district is committed to *continuous improvement*. 1–2–3.
7. The district assesses its *strengths and weaknesses*. 1–2–3.
8. The district created *informal classroom assessments* aligned to its instructional goals. 1–2–3.
9. The instructional program is *focused* on improving identified instructional issues. 1–2–3.
10. The *non-instructional components of the district support* student achievement. 1–2–3.
11. The district plans include a *multi-year plan* for improvement. 1–2–3.
12. The district *reviews procedures and processes* that impact student achievement. 1–2–3.

13. The *"day to day" work* of the district addresses student achievement. 1–2–3.
14. *Instructional programs* are improving student achievement. 1–2–3.
15. Leaders make the improvement of *student achievement a priority*. 1–2–3.
16. Leaders utilize *District and School Action Plans* to improve student achievement. 1–2–3.
17. District and School Action Plans are *effective* in improving student achievement. 1–2–3.
18. There is evidence that members of the district *understand its targets and outcomes*. 1–2–3.
19. There is a belief the district has the *internal capacity* to improve. 1–2–3.
20. There is an *expectation* that the district can overcome its student achievement issues. 1–2–3.
21. The district utilizes *instructional benchmarks* to assess its progress. 1–2–3.
22. The improvement process is *inclusive and collaborative*. 1–2–3.
23. The staff is *empowered* to create and implement solutions to problems. 1–2–3.
24. Staff members have an avenue to participate in *instructional decisions*. 1–2–3.
25. Staff members *understand* the parts of the plan which impact them. 1–2–3.

ATMOSPHERE/ATTITUDE/CULTURE

Focus: To build a culture of teamwork, collaboration, and positive attitude that maximizes the talents of employees in creating a high performing organization.

1. Staff members demonstrate the *values* of the organization. 1–2–3.
2. The district encourages *professional development*. 1–2–3.
3. *Adequate time* has been provided for collaboration. 1–2–3.
4. A *problem-solving framework* is utilized. 1–2–3.
5. District practices *empower* staff. 1–2–3.
6. New staff exhibit the *desired attitude*, personality, and aptitude. 1–2–3.
7. New staff possess *skills that align* with the district's challenges and goals. 1–2–3.
8. The *placement of staff* is based on skills and strengths. 1–2–3.
9. The district has the *"right people on the bus."* 1–2–3.
10. Staff members work *collaboratively* to meet district and building goals. 1–2–3.

11. The district is *a team* with all members working toward a common goal. 1–2–3.
12. There is a strong sense of *"buy-in"* in meeting goals. 1–2–3.
13. The district fosters a *mentoring and coaching* model for staff. 1–2–3.
14. The district supports a structured or *differentiated model* of professional development. 1–2–3.
15. The district supports a *"teacher leader"* model or program. 1–2–3.
16. A *career ladder* is provided for those teachers interested in leadership opportunities. 1–2–3.
17. Members of the organization are *recognized for performance* in the classroom. 1–2–3.
18. Staff members collaborate to improve *instructional practices*. 1–2–3.
19. *Professional development* is aligned with district goals and practices. 1–2–3.
20. The district provides *adequate resources* to improve achievement. 1–2–3.
21. A *"child-first" mantra* is pervasive. 1–2–3.
22. The organization views *instruction as its priority*. 1–2–3.
23. The staff *defers individual accolades* to one of group recognition. 1–2–3.
24. Leaders instill *confidence* that success is possible. 1–2–3.
25. There is a climate of *"shared responsibility."* 1–2–3.

ACCOUNTABILITY

Focus: To design a systemic, customized, continuous improvement model with measurable benchmark indicators and processes that monitor and adjust effectiveness.

1. The district consistently meets its *targeted outcomes*. 1–2–3.
2. The district has a *system of accountability*. 1–2–3.
3. The district holds *individuals accountable* for achievement results. 1–2–3.
4. The district has a *group system of accountability* (i.e., building, department, etc.). 1–2–3.
5. The district's system of *accountability motivates* me to improve student achievement. 1–2–3.
6. Data gathering is *focused* on student performance. 1–2–3.
7. The district has a *design* which includes achievement-focused goals. 1–2–3.
8. Goals and Expectations are *communicated*. 1–2–3.
9. Building Goals are *derived* from District Goals. 1–2–3.

10. All goals are measurable with *specific criteria*. 1–2–3.
11. Action Plans are *aligned* with district and/or building goals. 1–2–3.
12. *Multiple sources of data* (i.e., standardized tests, benchmarks, etc.) assess progress. 1–2–3.
13. Data is *reviewed quarterly and annually*. 1–2–3.
14. Data reports and summaries are provided to *staff and the community*. 1–2–3.
15. Data is utilized to make *adjustments* to instructional trendlines. 1–2–3.
16. Accountability includes *what* is taught, *how* it is taught, and student *results*. 1–2–3.
17. Accountability includes *teacher goals* which involve student progress. 1–2–3.
18. Classroom or *Action Research* is encouraged.
19. The system of accountability includes *supports* for struggling teachers. 1–2–3.
20. The evaluation process encourages *professional growth*. 1–2–3.
21. The staff is *proficient in measuring* student achievement. 1–2–3.
22. The staff is *proficient in the analysis of data and utilizes it* to improve achievement. 1–2–3.
23. The data system *links* student reports and student data to planning resources. 1–2–3.
24. *Classroom Observations* are helpful in improving performance. 1–2–3.
25. *Evaluations* provide feedback that improves performance. 1–2–3.

ADEPT LEADERSHIP

Focus: to develop a collaborative model which assists in aligning all aspects of the organization to achieve higher performance levels and excellence.

1. The leadership team facilitated the goal development process. 1–2–3.
2. The leadership reviewed long and short-term action plans. 1–2–3.
3. The leadership team reinforces the values and beliefs of the district. 1–2–3.
4. The leadership team, as part of a review process, eliminates ineffective programs. 1–2–3.
5. The leadership eliminates non-instructional distractions. 1–2–3.
6. The leadership is "laser-focused" on achievement and improvement. 1–2–3.
7. The leadership team influences the district's progress to improve. 1–2–3.
8. Flexibility is exhibited in implementing goals and action plans. 1–2–3.
9. Leaders are inclusive in the decision-making process. 1–2–3.

10. Leaders encourage "risk taking" or "out of the box" thinking. 1–2–3
11. Leaders engage all stakeholders (i.e., teachers, parents, etc.) in improvement process. 1–2–3.
12. Leaders seek additional resources to assist with the improvement process. 1–2–3.
13. Leaders reinforce teamwork. 1–2–3.
14. The leaders of the organization value the people within it. 1–2–3.
15. Leaders encourage staff members to grow professionally. 1–2–3.
16. The leaders are inclusive in its problem-solving process. 1–2–3.
17. The leadership team effectively communicates with all staff members. 1–2–3.
18. The leaders model the values, beliefs, and mission of the district. 1–2–3.
19. The leadership organized frameworks, structures, or processes to ensure success. 1–2–3.
20. Leaders assume responsibility for the success or shortcomings of the district. 1–2–3.
21. The leadership team has demonstrated expertise in the execution of goals. 1–2–3.
22. Leaders have developed well-articulated parent engagement programs. 1–2–3.
23. The leadership creates an environment for students and staff to succeed. 1–2–3.
24. The leadership team operates in a fair, equitable, and professional manner. 1–2–3.
25. Leaders recognize staff accomplishments. 1–2–3.

PART II DOCUMENT REVIEW AND ANALYSIS (OPTIONAL)

The document review component of the School Systems "Cross Check" Instrument examines and further analyzes the impact of school/district policies on student achievement and school/district effectiveness in the context of the four elements of Alignment, Atmosphere/Attitude, Accountability, and Adept Leadership.

The documents reviewed are as follows:

- Strategic Plans/School and District Goals.
- Human Resources Recruitment and Hiring.
- Curriculum and Programming.
- Instructional Practices and Methodology.
- System of Assessment and Achievement Data.

Appendix A: Performance Instruments and Tools 109

- Observation/Supervision and Evaluation Practices.
- Professional Development.
- Financial Planning: Priorities and Allocations.
- Communication.
- Board Policies.

A rubric is utilized to rate the quality of the document and practices in the context of how each contributes to student achievement and higher performance. The rubric has defined criteria which correlate to high performing schools and districts.

Each document is rated a "3" (the highest correlation to higher outcomes and instructional quality), a "2," or a "1" (which indicates the lowest correlation to higher outcomes and instructional quality).

DOCUMENT REVIEW RUBRIC

Ratings/Criteria

Directions: Rate the designated areas based on the following rubric:

3

- Documents and plans reflect current district strategic planning and thinking.
- Organizational documents align with organizational outcomes.
- Processes and practices are consistent with targeted goals and outcomes.
- The mission, vision, values, and beliefs are embedded.
- Best practices are represented in the documents, policies, and practices.
- Policies and practices contribute to an environment of "continuous improvement."
- An optimum learning environment is a result of quality practices and policies.
- Policies contribute to organizational effectiveness.
- Policies, practices, and documents contribute to a professional environment.

2

- Documents and plans are inconsistent in reflecting current district planning and thinking.
- Organizational documents sporadically align with organizational outcomes.
- Processes and practices are inconsistent with targeted goals and outcomes.
- The mission, vision, and beliefs are periodically mentioned in documents.
- Best practices are somewhat represented in the documents, practices, and policies.

- The documents, practices, and policies may contribute to "continuous improvement."
- The learning environment is less than ideal.
- Policies contributing to organizational effectiveness are not consistent in all areas.
- The professional environment is hindered by the district's practices and policies.

1

- Documents and plans do not reflect current district strategic planning and thinking.
- Organizational documents do not align with organizational outcomes.
- Processes and practices do not target desired goals and outcomes.
- Mission, vision, values, and belief statements are not represented in documents.
- There is no evidence of best practices in documents, policies, and practices.
- An environment of "continuous improvement" is non-existent.
- The learning environment is poor.
- Policies do not contribute to organizational effectiveness.
- A professional environment is non-existent.

DOCUMENT RATINGS

Strategic Plans/School and District Goals 1–2–3
Human Resources Recruitment and Hiring 1–2–3
Curriculum and Programming 1–2–3
Instructional Practices and Methodology 1–2–3
System of Assessment and Achievement Data 1–2–3
Observation/Supervision and Evaluation Practices 1–2–3
Professional Development 1–2–3
Financial: Budget Review/Priorities/Allocations 1–2–3
Communication 1–2–3
Board Policies 1–2–3

Notations:
_____
_____
_____

Average Score*: _____

* the score represents a guide to identifying policies and practices that are problematic in the school/district improvement process. (Exemplary Schools Organization)

School System "Cross Check"

Tabulations
Average Subtotal:

- Alignment _____
- Atmosphere/Attitude _____
- Accountability _____
- Adept Leadership _____

Total Average Score: _____
Level of Connectedness*:
Subtotal Average Ranking:

- High Level of Effectiveness: 64–75 (85th percentile +)
- Moderate Level of Effectiveness: 56–63 (75th–84th)
- Marginal Level of Effectiveness: 48–55 (64th–74th)
- Ineffective Level: 47 and below (63rd and below)

Total Average Ranking:

- High Level of Effectiveness: 255–300 (85th percentile+)
- Moderate Level of Effectiveness: 225–254 (75th–84th)
- Marginal Level of Effectiveness: 192–224 (64th–73rd)
- Ineffective Level: 189 and below (63rd and below)

* the subtotal and total are guides in determining the level of connectedness or disconnection within an organization.

A #2 HIERARCHY OF SCHOOL/DISTRICT DEVELOPMENT (REVISED EDITION 2019)

Focus: This informal instrument generates discussion among stakeholders regarding the current status of a school or district's achievement level.

Directions: Place a check mark next to the statements in each category if your school or district meets or exceeds the criteria stated.

CATEGORIZATION OF DEVELOPMENT LEVELS

WORLD CLASS

___ Achievement results correlate favorably to exemplary levels of performance on the "Program for International Student Assessment" (PISA) or Trends in International Mathematics and Science Study (TIMSS).

___ Student issues/needs, instruction, and learning are a priority.

___ High degree of professional creativity and collaboration.

___ Individualization and student learning plans are the norm.

___ Ranked among the top 5 schools or school districts in the state by the State Department of Education or surveys such as Forbes, US News & World Report.

___ Able to recruit and retain talented and experienced professionals.

___ meets criteria in all statements listed above; if criteria are met, do not proceed to the next category.

EXEMPLARY

___ School and/or School District scores at the highest levels on all state and national assessments (90th percentile on all state standardized assessments), National Assessment of Educational Progress (NAEP) and Scholastic Aptitude Testing (SAT) and Advanced Placement Tests (AP).

___ Executes a strategic *instructional* plan that improves student performance annually.

___ High degree of confidence permeates throughout the organization and for its planning to improve instruction and student performance.

___ School or district is respected regionally for its instructional program.

___ There is evidence of instructional relationships between grades and organizational levels (elementary, middle, high school).

___ Staff retention is high and applicants are abundant for *all* positions.

___ Meets five out of the six criteria listed above; if criteria are met, do not proceed to next category.

ADVANCING

___ School and/or school district has/have demonstrated continuous and steady growth on state and national assessments.
___ On an annual basis the school or district moves students from underperformance to proficiency.
___ Seeking solutions and refining initiatives in an effort to improve its achievement issues.
___ Building the school or district's internal professional capacity to address achievement issues.
___ Competitive in the recruitment process.
___ Meets five of the six criteria listed above; if criteria are met, do not proceed to the next category.

MAINTENANCE

___ School or school district results remain stagnant over several years or consistently fall below acceptable "cut offs" for performance at the state level.
___ Little focus on instructional improvement.
___ Strong deference to "tradition" and past practices regardless of success or failure.
___ Struggles to fill positions.
___ Survival issues are prevalent: funding, safety, retention, and enrollment are not stable, etc.
___ Goals are not met.
___ meeting any one or more of the criteria in this category.

A #3 MASTER TEACHER

Job Description

The responsibilities associated with the Master Teacher designation attempts to create a "community of learners" in which teachers are empowered to demonstrate and/or to provide leadership to their peers regarding "best practice," methodology, etc.

According to the agreement between the teacher's association and the School Board of Directors, the master teacher's additional responsibilities, including but not limited to the development and participation in an annual Best Practices Fair, are providing leadership on district committees, assisting in the implementation of the Mentoring and Induction Program, attending designated staff development programs, and filling vacancies as team leader (middle school), department chairs, and elementary curriculum specialists.

Periodic release time as needed may be required to accomplish the aforementioned responsibilities. Other activities defined by the applicant, consistent with district initiatives and approved by the superintendent, can also comprise one's duties.

Responsibilities include but may not be limited to the following:

- Participation in Best Practices Fair
- Organizing and/or Leading Professional Development Sessions
- Providing Leadership on District Committees
- Acting as Demonstration Teacher for District Teachers
- Formal and/or Informal Mentoring of Non-Tenured Teachers
- Primary Project Leader on a Study Topic
- Summer Curriculum Writing/Curriculum Revision Activities

It should be noted that this appointment is a non-supervisory position with evaluative authority.

The position is a non-permanent position with a term of two years.

An application must be completed and one's application must be favorably reviewed by your assigned building principal prior to district office review.

MASTER TEACHER—CRITERIA/ APPLICATION PROCESS

Criteria

- Instructional II Certification (Permanent Endorsement)

- Evaluation
  - Satisfactory Final Ratings in All Categories (Minimum Five Consecutive Years)
  - No "Needs Improvement" Ratings Recorded (Last Five Years)
- Pathways Participation (Classroom Goal Setting)
  - Two Consecutive Years
- Leadership
  - Committee Participation: Building and/or District Level
  - Conference Workshop Attendance
  - Curriculum Writing
  - Formal/Informal Mentoring of Teachers
  - Demonstration Lessons of Best Practices

Application Process

- Submit Cover Application by (Spring of Each Year)
- Supplemental Information
  - Pathways Classroom Goal Plan (Two Years)
  - Principal Recommendation
  - Exemplary Observation Reports (Five Consecutive Reports)
- Written Response: Describe Why You Are a Master Teacher (Refer to Framework of Skills and Knowledge Standards Rubric in Pathways Document)
- Teach a Demonstration Lesson to Selection Committee Representatives

Submission Process

- By (select date), submit the application and Requested Information in a binder to the superintendent of schools.
- Binder should be organized as follows:
  - Principal recommendation
  - Last five years of final evaluations
  - Pathways action research project
  - Summary of leadership roles
- Plan of a Model Lesson with All Key Components
- Observational reports (last five years)

- Written response to master teacher question (see above)
- Demonstration lesson
  - Selection/Observation Committee Chair will schedule observation

DISPUTES

- All issues regarding the application process will be resolved by the District Improvement Team prior to formal submission of the application to the superintendent of schools.

FINAL SELECTION

- The superintendent makes the final selection of master teachers. All decisions are final and not subject to appeal.

A #4 OBSERVATION/SUPERVISION STRATIFICATION LIST

Focus: To provide a stratified or tiered level of support to teachers by delineating the number of observations per staff member based on the individual functioning or developmental level.

Guidelines:

1. Observations must be conducted within the framework of existing contractual obligations regarding the formal observation and supervision process. Notification and written feedback must be provided in accordance with district procedures and the agreement between the teacher association and the board of directors.
2. New teachers will be formally observed by the building principal or their designee a minimum of three times per year.
3. Teachers on intervention will be interviewed a minimum of three times per year by the building principal or their designee along with additional observations provided as necessary by mentors or coaches.
4. Teachers with satisfactory evaluations at the conclusion of the previous school year will be observed a minimum of two times per year by the building principal or their designee.
5. Teachers with an exemplary evaluative rating from the previous year will be observed one time per year by the building principal or their designee.

Procedure:

1. Submit the school or building's observational schedule to the assistant superintendent for curriculum and instruction or the superintendent.
2. The observation/supervision stratification list should include a list of teachers under the following headings:
   - One observation
   - Two observations
   - Three observations (include reason for the listing)

A #5 TRIAGE LIST: STUDENTS

Focus: The list is designed to focus staff efforts on those students who are failing, marginal, or below proficiency.

	Student Name	Teacher	Reading Score	Math Score	Intervention	Monitor
1						
2						
3						
4						
5						
6						
7						
8						
9						

Procedure:

1. Principal facilitates the development of the list prior to building/school goal and action plan submission for review at the district level. There is no limitation on the number of students listed, but the principal and the Building Improvement Team should be cognizant of the finite number of resources available.
2. The number of intensive interventions per pupil is determined by the Building/School Improvement Team.
3. The number of students on the list correlates with the targeted percentage of growth required in a designated year.

A #6 BOARD OF DIRECTORS/ADMINISTRATOR RETREAT FRAMEWORK

AGENDA

Day 1: Board and Administrators

Participants: Board Members, Principals

I. District Reports

   A. State of the district report: Composed and delivered by the superintendent.
   B. School and building reports: Principals.
   C. District data review: Assistant superintendent or appropriate administrator.

II. Appreciative Inquiry

   A. Each board member and administrator discusses the positives of the district.
   B. The facilitator (superintendent or designee) interprets remarks and each group's statements by category (Achievement, Community Outreach, Personalization, Staff, Facilities, etc.).
   C. Distribute five blue, five yellow, and five red posted notes to each board member and administrator.
   D. Rank listed categories on colored "posted notes" according to the following guide:

   - Blue color signifies the highest rating.
   - Yellow signifies the second highest rating.
   - Red signifies the lowest rating.

   E. Each board member and administrator places their color posted notes on poster paper on the retreat room walls.

III. Tabulations

   A. Each colored posted note is given a value as follows:

   - Blue = 5 points
   - Yellow = 3 points
   - Red = 1 points

   B. Value by category is tabulated.
   C. Discussion about each category's total ranking.

D. Categories are regrouped/consolidated and placed under specific areas within a school or district (i.e., Curriculum and Instruction, Personnel and Human Relations, Finance, Technology, etc.).

IV. Consolidated Category Discussion

A. Board Members and Administrators are equally distributed to form groups to discuss the categories and the ranking with the goal of providing specific recommendations for improvement.

B. Each committee reports to the group as to areas of general consensus that aim at improvement.

Day 2

Participants: Board Members and Cabinet Members

I. Cabinet and Board Committee Reports
- Finance
- Personnel and Human Relations
- Curriculum and Instruction
- Student and Community Affairs
- Technology
- Pupil Personnel and Special Education

II. Board Member and Cabinet Goal Development
III. Legal Updates (Presentation by District Solicitor)
IV. Contemporary Topics (Superintendent and Cabinet)
V. Summary and Closure*

* Superintendent complies a written summary of data and feedback for distribution to the board and administrators.

Appendix A: Performance Instruments and Tools

A #7 BOARD OF DIRECTORS/ADMINISTRATOR RETREAT FRAMEWORK

ALTERNATIVE AGENDA

Day 1

Participants: Board, Superintendent, Cabinet, Principals.

I. District Reports

    A. Opening Video
    B. Program Review: Superintendent provides the board with report of district progress regarding initiatives.

II. Discussion

    A. Activity #1: Delivering 21st Century Skills

        1. What 21st century skills will students require?
        2. Are some skills more important than others?
        3. What does research indicate?

    B. Activity #2: Delivering 21st Century Skills

        1. How will the schools and the district measure the effectiveness of skill delivery?
        2. How will the schools and the district measure skill acquisition?
        3. As a district, do we deliver 21st century skills?
        4. What skills seem underemphasized?

Day 2

Participants: School Board, Superintendent, Cabinet.

I. Prioritize Challenge: All participants review discussions from previous day and determine priorities.
II. Cabinet Reports: Projecting future issues and trends

    A. Curriculum: Keeping ahead of the curve—responding to trends, indicators, and data
    B. Finance: Declining revenues and increasing demands
    C. Pupil Services: Focusing on individual student needs
    D. Technology: Staying current but not going off the edge
    E. Facilities: Adjusting to change: Keeping the district's form functional

F. Community Relations/Student Life: Keeping it personal
   G. Safety and Wellness: Proactivity and prevention
III. Governance: Superintendent discusses any pertinent issues with the board.
IV. Superintendent: Building a future for students together.

Appendix B:
Leadership Development Exercises

B #1 "WARRIOR OR WIZARD"

I. List issues or obstacles which you as a leader resolved in the last year.

1. _____
2. _____
3. _____
4. _____
5. _____

II. List the attributes of the "Warrior" Leader.

1. _____
2. _____
3. _____

III. List the attributes of a "Wizard" Leader.

1. _____
2. _____
3. _____

IV. Cite a time when you were a "Warrior" and when you were a "Wizard."
V. Cite a time when you were simultaneously both a "Warrior" and a "Wizard."

B #2 "NORTH STAR"

Focus: Leaders will reflect upon their beliefs and guiding principles through an interactive exercise.

  I. Distribute a mini-compass to each participant. Orient participants in the utilization of the compass.
 II. Pre-select key landmarks in your area and have each leader attempt to locate them with the compass.
III. Have each part participant record the coordinates of the landmarks in degrees.
 IV. Discuss the process which was utilized in locating the landmark. (Hint: Must establish the magnetic north or "true north" on the compass.)
  V. Have each leader list their "True North" which guides them.
 VI. Develop a list of school or district's beliefs.

   1. _____
   2. _____
   3. _____
   4. _____
   5. _____

 VII. Have each leader provide evidence of the existence of the above belief systems in their school or district.
VIII. Discuss if the school or district adheres to those beliefs.
  IX. Have each leader provide a location in their school or district to display the compass.

B #3 "ICEBERG IS MELTING"

Background: Based on John Kotter's "Our Iceberg Is Melting," the dynamics of change is explored below:

A. List the factors that impact student achievement and school performance.

1. _____
2. _____
3. _____
4. _____
5. _____

B. How do you plan to overcome those issues listed above?

1. _____
2. _____
3. _____
4. _____
5. _____

C. What is your plan to build support to overcome those obstacles?
D. How do you handle those staff members that refuse to "buy-in" to the school's strategy?
E. Is there a time when a leader moves forward without the consensus of the faculty and staff?

B #4 SYNERGISTIC OR STRATEGIC

List leadership moments or situations when you have demonstrated a synergistic style of leadership.

1. _____
2. _____
3. _____
4. _____
5. _____

List leadership duties or tasks that require strategic thinking or maneuvering.

1. _____
2. _____
3. _____
4. _____
5. _____

Explain how the combination of synergistic principles and strategies produce positive outcomes in your current position.

How does focusing on the internal capacity of an organization build synergy?

B #5 GUIDING PRINCIPLES

The five principles listed below provide a guideline in the implementation of a reform agenda that focuses on improving student achievement and school performance.

Under each guideline, provide at least three ways which, as a leader, you can apply in your current or future position.

"Child First Focus"

1. _____
2. _____
3. _____

Systemic

1. _____
2. _____
3. _____

Analytical

1. _____
2. _____
3. _____

Instructional

1. _____
2. _____
3. _____

Measurable

1. _____
2. _____
3. _____

B #6 CRITIQUE OF HIRING PROCESS

Reflection:

I. Take a moment to reflect upon the hiring practices in one's school or district. Some areas of consideration include:

- What criteria are utilized in the application screening process?
- Who develops the criteria?
- Who participates in the hiring process?
- What colleges and universities provide a majority of the school or district's applicants?
- Does the school or district fill vacancies with highly talented individuals?
- Do the applicants' skills and experiences match those needed by the school and district?
- What characteristics does the school or district consider a priority in the hiring process?
- When assigning new staff to a school, is the chemistry within the organization a consideration?

II. Examine the school or district's strengths and weaknesses.
III. How would you improve the recruitment and hiring process?

B #7 "MANDATE TO IMPROVE"

Scenario:

I. You are interviewed by the School Board of Directors for the position of superintendent. From the outset of the interview, the board is clear that the next superintendent must improve student achievement and performance in the district.

Associated with the challenge of school/district improvement, the board wants to know if your management style is compatible with the challenge of reversing the on-going trend of declining achievement.

Explain to the board, as leader of the district, how you will:

- Instill Confidence;
- Facilitate Change;
- Demonstrate Determination;
- Share Responsibility.

II. In responding to the board, outline a framework that you will utilize in the improvement process.

B #8 "80–20" RULE

The "Pareto Principle" states that for many events, roughly 80% of the effects come from 20% of the causes.

When examining the dilemma of student achievement in the schools, the "Pareto Principle" is viewed as identifying 20% of teaching practices, policies, and procedures which may contribute to 80% of the learning.

Take a moment to reflect on what that 20% might be and list those items below:

1. _____
2. _____
3. _____
4. _____
5. _____
6. _____
7. _____
8. _____
9. _____
10. _____

B #9 BUILDING AND DISTRICT GOALS/ACTION PLANS

Instructions:

I. Based on an identified instructional deficiency that is impacting student achievement and school/district performance, develop a plan to rectify the deficiency by writing a district goal and subsequent action plan.

Be cognizant that the goal must be measurable and the action plan specific in term of its execution (i.e., responsibility for goal monitoring and timeline for completion).

District Goal:

_____

Action Plan

1. _____
2. _____
3. _____
4. _____
5. _____

II. Convert the goal and action plan to one that extends to the building or school level.

Building Goal:

_____

Action Plan

1. _____
2. _____
3. _____
4. _____
5. _____

B #10 CASE STUDY ANALYSIS

Instructions:

Examine both Case Studies and make a comprehensive list of elements, components, and instructional items that may be helpful in creating a plan to improve performance in a school or school district.

1. _____
2. _____
3. _____
4. _____
5. _____
6. _____
7. _____
8. _____
9. _____
10. _____
11. _____
12. _____
13. _____
14. _____
15. _____

Notes

PREFACE

1 Lauren Camera, "NAEP Shows Little to No Gains in Math, Reading for U.S. Students," *U S News and World Report*, accessed April 10, 2018, https://usnews.com/topics/author/lauren-camera.

2. Eric A. Hanushek, Paul E. Peterson, and Ludger Woessmann, *Endangering Prosperity: A Global View of the American School*, foreword by Lawrence H. Summers (Washington, DC: Brookings Institute Press, 2013), 8.

3. Louis Serino, "What International Test Scores Reveal about American Education?" *The Brown Center Chalkboard* (blog), Brookings Institute, April 2017, https://www.brookings.edu/brown-center-chalkboard/2017/04/07/17/what-international-test scores-reveal-about-american-education/.

4. Catherine Gewertz, "Math Scores Slide to 20-Year Low on ACT," *Education Week* 38(2018): 7.

INTRODUCTION

1. Eric A. Hanushek, Paul E. Peterson, and Ludger Woessmann, *Endangering Prosperity: A Global View of the American School*, foreword by Lawrence H. Summers (Washington, DC: Brookings Institute Press, 2013), 8.

CHAPTER 1

1. Camera, "NAEP Shows Little to No Gains in Math, Reading for U.S. Students," 1–2.

2. US Department of Education, "Improving Basic Programs Operated by Local Education Agencies (Title I, Part A)," Program Description, Washington, DC., last modified October 24, 2018, https://www.2.ed.gov/titleiparta/index.htm/.

3. Ibid.

4. John Merrow, *Choosing Excellence: Good Schools Are Not Good Enough* (Lanham, MD: Scarecrow Press, 2001).

5. Michael J. Petrilli, "Where Education Reform Goes from Here," *Education Next* (July 12, 2018), http://www.educationnext.org/where-education-reform-goes-here/.

6. CBS News, "How Schools Work," *Face the Nation*, John Dickerson interviewing Arne Duncan, April 5, 2018, http://cbsnews.com/transcrpits-arne-duncan-on-face-the-nation-auguest-5-2018.

7. Ibid.

CHAPTER 2

1. Robert Porter Lynch, "Synergy or Synchronicity: How the Synergistic Leader Builds Powerful Alliance Relationships," *Synergistic Leader* (blog), 2002.

2. Dave McKeown, *The Synergist: How to Lead Your Team to Predictable Success* (New York: St. Martin's Press, 2012).

3. Lee G. Bolman and Terrence E. Deal, *The Wizard and the Warrior: Leading with Passion and Power* (San Francisco: Jossey-Bass, 2006), 163–65.

CHAPTER 3

1. National Institute of Standards and Technology, *Baldrige Excellence Framework 2017–2018 (Education)*, Gaithersburg, MD. Last modified January 12, 2017, https://nist.gov.

2. Lawrence W. Lezotte and Barbara C. Jacoby, *Sustainable School Reform: The District Context for Improvement* (Okemos, MI: Effective Schools Products, 1991), 238–45.

3. Heidi Hayes Jacobs, *Getting Results with Curriculum Mapping* (Alexandria, VA: Association of Supervision and Curriculum Development, 2004).

4. Andi Stix, "Essential and Guiding Questions," *Stix Picks for the Interactive Classroom* (blog), April 29, 2012, https://andistix.com.

5. Grant Wiggins and Jay McTighe, *Understanding by Design* (Alexandria, VA: ASCD, 2004).

6. Robert J. Marzano, David C. Yanoski, Jan K. Hoegh, and Julia A. Simms, *Using Common Core Standards* (Centennial, CO: Marzano Research, 2013).

7. Jeff Colosimo, Eduplanet 21-Curriculum Software Design Company, 2018, https://www.eduplanet21.com.

8. Robert J. Marzano, *What Works in Schools: Translating Research into Action* (Alexandria, VA: ASCD, 2003).

9. John Doerr, *Measure What Matters: How Google, Bono, and the Gates Rock the World with OKR's* (New York: Penguin Random House, 2017), 7.

10. Doerr, 10.

11. Doerr, 12.
12. Doerr, 15.

CHAPTER 4

1. National Academy of Sciences, *"Gallup Teacher Perceiver Instrument Appendix E,"* www.nap.edu/read/1043/chap12.
2. Donald Merle Chalker, "The Teacher Perceiver as an Instrument for Predicting Successful Teacher Behavior," *Research Gate*, 2018, https://www.researchgate.net/publication/241840845.
3. Colin L. Powell and Tony Koltz, *It Works for Me: In Life and Leadership* (New York: Harper Perennial, 2012), 279.
4. Scott Beare and Michael McMillan, *The Power of Teamwork* (Naperville, IL: Simple Truths, 2006), 54–55.
5. Patrik Jonsson, "America's Biggest Teacher and Principal Cheating Scandal Unfolds in Atlanta," https://www.csmonitor.com/USA/Education/2011/0705/America-s.
6. Taylor Torregano, "Testimony Ties Saunders to Manatee Graduation Rates," *Herald Tribune*, January 2, 2019, https://www.heraldtribune.com/news/20190102/testimony_ties.
7. Jay Wright, Michael Sheridan, and Dan Dacostino, *Attitude: Develop a Winning Mindset on and off the Court* (New York: Ballantine Books-Penguin Random House, 2017).

CHAPTER 5

1. Michael Fullan, *The New Meaning of Educational Change* (New York/London: Teachers College, Columbia University, 2001), 75–94.
2. Michael Fullan, *Change Forces: The Sequel* (Philadelphia: Farmer Press, 1999), ix.
3. Vincent F. Cotter and Robert D. Hassler, *Performance Is Key: Connecting the Links to Leadership and Excellence* (Lanham, MD: Rowman and Littlefield, 2017).
4. National Institute of Standards and Technology, *Baldridge Excellence Framework 2017–2018 (Education)*, Gaithersburg, MD, last modified January 12, 2017, https://nist.gov.
5. Lawrence W. Lezotte and Barbara C. Jacoby, *Sustainable School Reform: The District Context for School Improvement* (Okemos, MI: Effective Schools Products, 1991).
6. John Doerr, *Measure What Matters: How Google, Bono and the Gates Foundation Rock the World with OKR's* (New York: Penguin Random House, 2018).
7. Colin L. Powell and Tony Koltz, *It Works for Me: In Life and Leadership* (New York: Harper Perennial, 2012), 169.

CHAPTER 6

1. Eric H. Kessler, *The Appreciative Inquiry Model: Encyclopedia of Management Publications* (Los Angeles, CA: Sage Publications, 2013), www.gervasebushe.ca/the_AI_model.pdf.
2. *Hanover Research Report*, "Best Practices for School Improvement Planning, Hanover Research," Washington, DC, October 2014, 14, www.hanoverresearch.com/media/best-practices-for-School-Improvement-Planning.
3. Kevin Kruse, "The 80/20 Rule and How It Can Change Your Life, *Forbes*, May 7, 2016, https://www.forbes.com/sites/KevinKruse/2016/03/07/80-20rule.

CHAPTER 7

1. *Hanover Research Report*, "Best Practices for School Improvement Plan, Hanover Research, Washington, DC, October 2014, 5, www.hanoverresearch.com/meida/best-practices-for-School-Improvement-Planning.

CHAPTER 8

1. Richard F. Elmore, "Bridging the Gap between Standards and Achievement: The Imperative for Professional Development in Education," *Albert Shanker Institute*, 2002, 26, archived at https://www.shankerinstitute.org/site/shanker/files/Bridging__Gap.pdf.
2. Denisa R. Superville, "Principals Say Coaching Not Compliance Is What They Need from Central Office," *Education Week* (blog), July 10, 2018, https://www.edweek.org/edweek.
3. Marilyn Katzenmeyer and Gayle Moller, *Awakening the Sleeping Giant* (Thousand Oaks, CA: Corwin Press, Inc., 2001), 2.
4. Roland S. Barth, *Learning by Heart* (San Francisco, CA: Jossey-Bass, 2004), 117.

CHAPTER 9

1. John Jay Bonstingl, "The Quality Revolution in Education," *Educational Leadership*, 50, no. 3 (November 1992), 4–9.
2. David J. Kirk and Terry L. Jones, "Effective Schools," *Pearson Assessment Report* (July 2004), 2–7.

Bibliography

Barth, Roland S. *Learning by Heart*. San Francisco: Jossey-Bass, 2004.
Beare, Scott, and Michael McMillan. *The Power of Teamwork*. Naperville, IL: Simple Truths, 2006.
Bolman, Lee G., and Terrence E. Deal. *The Wizard and the Warrior: Leading with Passion and Power*. San Francisco: Jossey-Bass, 2006.
Bonstingl, John Jay. "The Quality Revolution in Education." *Educational Leadership* 50, no. 3 (November 1992).
Camera, Lauren. "NAEP Shows Little to No Gains in Math, Reading for U.S. Students." *US News and World Report* (blog). April 10, 2018. https://www.usnews.com/topics/author/lauren-camera.
CBS News. "How Schools Work." John Dickerson with Arne Duncan on *Face the Nation*, filmed on April 5, 2018. https://cbsnews.com/transcript-arne-duncan-on-face-the-nation-august-5-2018.
Chalker, Donald Merle. "The Teacher Perceiver as an Instrument for Predicting Successful Teacher Behavior." *Research Gate*. 2018. https://www.researchgate.net/publication/241840845
Colosimo, Jeff. Eduplanet21-Curriculum Design Software Company. 2018. https://www.eduplanet21.com
Cotter, Vincent F., and Robert D. Hassler. *Performance Is Key: Connecting the Links to Leadership and Excellence*. Lanham, MD: Rowman and Littlefield, 2017.
Doerr, John. *Measure What Matters: How Google, Bono, and the Gates Foundation Rock the World with OKR's*. New York: Penguin Random House, 2018.
Elmore, Richard F. "Bridging the Gap between Standards and Achievement: The Imperative for Professional Development in Education." *Albert Shanker Institute*, 2002. https://www.shankerinstitute.org/site/shanker/files/Bridging__Gap.pdf.
Fullan, Michael. *The New Meaning of Educational Change*. New York/London: Teachers College, Columbia University, 2001.
Fullan, Michael. *Change Forces: The Sequel*. Philadelphia: Farmer Press, 1999.

Gewertz, Catherine. "Math Scores Slide to 20-Year Low on ACT." *Education Week* 38 (2018), 7.

Hanover Research Report. "Best Practices for School Improvement Planning." Hanover Research, Washington, DC. https://www.hanoverresearch.com/media/Best-Practices-for-School-Improvement-Planning.

Hanushek, Eric A., Paul E. Peterson, and Ludger Woessman. *Endangering Prosperity: A Global View of the American School*. Foreword by Lawrence H. Summers. Washington, DC: Brookings Institute Press, 2013.

Jacobs, Heidi Hayes. *Getting Results with Curriculum Mapping*. Alexandria, VA: Association of Supervision and Curriculum Development (ASCD). 2004.

Jonsson, Patrik. "America's Biggest Teacher and Principal Cheating Scandal Unfolds in Atlanta." *The Christian Science Monitor*. July 5, 2011. https://www.csmonitor.com/USA/Education/2001/0705/America-s.

Katzenmeyer, Marilyn, and Gayle Moller. *Awakening the Sleeping Giant*. Thousand Oaks, CA: Corwin Press, Inc., 2001.

Kessler, Eric H. *Encyclopedia of Management Publications: Appreciative Inquiry*. Los Angeles, CA: Sage Publications, 2013.

Kirk, David J. "Effective Schools." *Pearson Assessment Report*. July 2017. Pearson-assessments.com/images/tmrs_rg/EffectiveSchools.pdf.

Kruse, Kevin. "The 80/20 Rule and How It Can Change Your Life." *Forbes*. 2016. https://forbes.com/sites/KevinKruse/2016/03/07/80-20rule.

Lezotte, Lawrence W., and Barbara C. Jacoby. *Sustainable School Reform: The District Context for School Improvement*. Okemos, MI: Effective Schools Products, 1991.

Lynch, Robert Porter. "Synergy or Synchronicity: How the Synergistic Leader Builds Powerful Alliance Relationships." *Synergistic Leader* (blog). 2002. https://www.synergisticleader.com/index.html.

Marzano, Robert J., David C. Yanoski, Jan K. Hoegh, and Julia A. Simms. *Using Common Core Standards to Enhance Instructional Assessment*. Centennial, Colorado: Marzano Research, 2013.

Marzano, Robert J. *What Works in Schools: Translating Research into Action*. Alexandria, VA: Association for Supervision and Curriculum Development, 2003.

McKeown, Dave. *The Synergist: How to Lead Your Team to Predictable Success*. New York: St. Martin's Press, 2012.

Merrow, John. *Choosing Excellence: Good Enough Schools Are Not Good Enough*. Lanham, MD: Scarecrow Press, 2001.

National Academy of Sciences. *Gallup Teacher Perceiver Instrument*, Appendix E. www.nap.edu/read/1043/chapter 12.

National Institute of Standards and Technology. *Baldrige Excellence Framework (Education)*. Gaithersburg, MD. Last modified January 12, 2017, https://nist.gov.

Petrilli, Michael J. "Where Education Reform Goes from Here," *Education Next*. (July 12, 2018). https://www.educationnext.org/where-education-goes-here.

Powell, Colin L., and Tony Koltz. *It Worked for Me: In Life and Leadership*. New York: Harper Perennial, 2012.

Serino, Louis. "What International Test Scores Reveal about American Education?" *The Brown Center Chalkboard* (blog). Brookings Institute. April 2017. https://www.brookings.edu/Brown-center-chalkboard/2017/04/07/17/what-international-testscores-reveal-about-american-education.

Stix, Andi. "Essential and Guiding Questions." *Stix Picks for the Interactive Classroom* (blog). April 29, 2012. https://andistix.com.

Superville, Denisa R. "Principals Say Coaching, Not Compliance, Is What They Need from Central Office." *Education Week* (blog). July 10, 2018. https://www.edweek.org./edweek.

US Department of Education, "Improving Basic Programs Operated by Local Agencies (Title I, Part A)." Washington, DC: Department of Education, 2018.

Wiggins, Grant, and Jay McTighe. *Understanding by Design*. Alexandria, VA: Association for Supervision and Curriculum, 2004.

Wright, Jay, Michael Sheridan, and Mark Dacostino. *Attitude: Develop a Winning Mindset on and off the Court*. New York: Ballantine Books-Penguin Random House, 2017.

About the Author

With over forty years in the field of education, Dr. Vincent F. Cotter, EdD, served as a teacher, department chair, and administrator in both urban and urban-suburban public schools. As superintendent of schools for eleven consecutive years, he was the primary innovator of a unique program, Reaching Above and Beyond, which dramatically improved student achievement. For his efforts, Dr. Cotter was awarded the prestigious American Society for Quality's international Juran Medal (2010) in the field of education for sustained systemic improvement.

Dr. Cotter has also written graduate level courses for aspiring principals and superintendents, provided consultative services to school districts, and cofounded the Exemplary Schools Organization. "Performance Is Key: Connecting the Links to Leadership and Excellence" was coauthored by Dr. Cotter and published by Rowman and Littlefield in 2017.

www.ingramcontent.com/pod-product-compliance
Lightning Source LLC
Chambersburg PA
CBHW030141240426
43672CB00005B/221